ALL-AGE SERVICES

All-Age Services

including 12 designs
for exploring the Bible together

BOB HARTMAN

David C Cook

First published 2009

Published by David C. Cook
Kingsway Communications Ltd
26–28 Lottbridge Drove, Eastbourne BN23 6NT, UK

David C. Cook
4050 Lee Vance View, Colorado Springs, CO 80918, USA

David C. Cook Distribution Canada
55 Woodslee Avenue, Paris, Ontario, Canada N3L 3E5

David C. Cook and the graphic circle C logo
are registered trademarks of Cook Communications Ministries.

ISBN 978 1 84291 393 2

Cover design by PinnacleCreative.co.uk

1 2 3 4 5 6 printing 12 11 10 09
Printed in Italy

Contents

Introduction

It's all about making a journey. Worship, that is. From A to Z. From here to there. Movement. Transition. Discovery.

And that's the problem some people have with all-age services. They don't think they 'go' anywhere. That's not how they express it, of course. They talk about them not being 'serious' enough. They complain that they are nothing more than a collection of children's activities. And in response, people like you and me, who lead all-age services, moan about these people's traditional ways and their unwillingness to try something new and their selfishness where worship is concerned, and ultimately end up quoting that passage about Jesus welcoming the children in an exasperated 'you're on the wrong side of that argument, buster!' kind of way. So there!

We don't usually conduct that argument out loud, of course. And seldom in the immediate direction of the person concerned. We grumble and they grumble, but the reality is that there is a solution. At least I think there is. And the solution lies in 'story'.

'There's nothing new about that,' you say. And if you mean dropping a story into the mix along with a lot of other activities, you're probably right. But that's not what I mean when I say that story is the answer to this problem – the problem of journeying in all-age services.

Story is the solution when we move from using it as one of the elements of the service to making it the framework of the service itself. When we begin the service where the story begins – at the 'once upon a time' moment, for lack of a better phrase – and when we bring the service to an end at 'happily ever after'. When we pray at those points in the story where it is appropriate to pray; where the story tells us to pray. And when we do the same with all the other elements we associate with worship: singing and dancing and preaching and meditating. We let the story be the guide, because it's God story, because the form we have the story in was inspired by his Holy Spirit. And we follow the story, from beginning to end, because every story is a journey. From A to Z. From here to there. Movement. Transition. Discovery.

Finally, because stories can be accessed at different levels of understanding, we let the story do its work for every age, as it is received. It's the story that brings us all together. And that's what an all-age service should be about. So you will find no instructions to gather the children at the front in this book. That merely excludes everyone else and communicates that what is happening is not for them. No, everything in these services is for everybody. If there is an activity where the bigger group breaks into smaller groups or into pairs, the assumption is that children and teens and adults will all be working together, talking or praying or drawing. All in the same boat. All engaged with the same story. All making the same journey.

And what is your job? If you are leading the service, then you are more like an orchestra conductor or a ringmaster than a preacher or teacher. You are moving the story along, weaving the elements together, clarifying any confusion, steering the boat. So you need to understand all the elements as and when they appear, but you don't have to do or lead them all. There is something much more interesting about a variety of voices than just one voice going on for an hour or so. So build yourself a team of helpers to do this with you: to be those alternating voices; to encourage audience participation, where needed; to dance, to act, to explain; to pass out supplies. Whatever is needed, because you won't be able to do this on your own.

So where are we going? Well, each story has its own narrative arc – from the first day of creation to the seventh. From the call of Abraham to the birth of Isaac. From the roof being wrecked to the man being healed. That sort of thing. This then calls to mind our own stories and invites us to travel along their paths as well.

But there is another story, an even bigger story that we will journey through. There are twelve services described in the book, and if you start the first one in June and do one a month, you will reach the Christmas story in December and the Easter story in April and you will have engaged with God's Big Story in the course of that year. My work in schools has shown me that most children don't understand the connection between the Bible stories they hear. But I am afraid that that is true for many adults as well – and I mean Christian adults! They have never had the big picture fitted together so that they can see the links and really appreciate the scope of God's work. This book attempts to address that, and while you are free to pick and choose and do the stories in any order you like (because, hey, you paid for it!) you and your church will get the most out of it if you follow the stories in order (because, hey, I wrote it!).

So tell your church what you're up to here. People always respond better when they know why something is happening. (I've been on plenty of delayed flights and stuck in loads of traffic jams, so I know!) Tell them it's new and it's different, but it's biblical to the core and it seeks only to bring people of all ages into contact with the best and biggest story of all: the story of how much God loves us and all that he has done for us because of that love. And if you make it sound really scary, they'll no doubt say, 'That wasn't nearly as frightening/bizarre/heretical as I thought it would be!'

So here are the stories. Use them as you find them. Adapt them and adjust them to suit your needs. And if you make a change that really works for you, let me know. Same goes for any joke you improve on. And if you are inspired by this to write a few story-services of your own, I'd especially like to have a look. That would be incredibly encouraging.

That's enough for now, I think. Have a look. Have a go. And may this 'once upon a time' all-age service approach be a 'happily ever after' experience for you!

Using this book

Each of the twelve stories starts with a summary of the preparation you will need to do in advance, the equipment you need to collect together and an outline of the service. Then the story is developed, explaining in detail how to shape it into a service. Finally a script for the service, including the story, is provided, which you may photocopy for ease of use if you wish.

Symbols are used to help you find your way easily around the services:

 Equipment you need to collect in advance

 Introduction

 Story

 Teaching

 Activity

 Prayer

 Songs

Which songs? Well, everyone's worship and song language is different, isn't it? I don't know which songs you know, and this probably isn't the best time to teach a lot of songs (well, all right then, you can teach one, if it really ties into the theme). I would suggest, however, that you use a mix of 'children's songs' and songs that might normally be sung by adults but whose words are simple enough for many of the children to understand. If you visit the Familyministry.co.uk website you will find a list of possible songs for each of the twelve stories. Let us know if something else works well for you and we'll add it to the list.

CREATION

In advance

Band to prepare appropriate music.

Craft materials, including lengths of cloth (coloured sheets?).

Outline

1st Start with God

God's creative power and majesty

Acknowledging God's power

Days of creation

Creation (Genesis 1), with display of activity

Praise for God's creation

God created us to have a good relationship with him

Thanks to God

Praise for God's creation

1st   Julie Andrews was absolutely right. Starting at the very beginning is, indeed, a very good place to start. So that's where our journey begins. Quite literally 'in the beginning'. There are a couple of things you want to aim for. You want your group to understand the story: what it means for them and for all the stories to come. But you also want them to 'feel' the story: to be drawn into its wonder and beauty and awe. The telling of the story, therefore, needs to be a kind of celebration, a glorious cacophony of sound and colour that reflects the bigness and brightness (and maybe even the messiness) of all that God has made for us. Now if your church (or your leadership team, or your senior pastor, or Mrs Perkins who sits three rows from the back and is constantly frowning) frets about noise and chaos in all-age services, you might want to warn them about what's coming. Better still, here is a simple 'noise management' tip that has (almost!) always worked for me.

When you introduce the story, tell people that some of them will be making noises and that they can (and should) be as loud as they like. But also tell them that when you stick your hand in the air, they need to get quiet as quickly as possible (immediately is good) so that you can move on to the next part of the story. Practise this with them if you have any doubts. Noise – Hand in air – Quiet. This little bit of 'control' will make everybody happy, and help to move the story along.

As it happens, however, you don't want to start with the story. You want to start with God. Because that's where the story starts: God, just God, Father, Son and Spirit, before anything was made.

🎵   While it's true that we don't have many worship songs about 'God, just God' (largely because we can only know him through our relationship with him and all that he has done), it would be appropriate to start by singing about him and to him, probably with a song or two that deals with his majesty, his love or his creative power.

🙏   A prayer would be nice after that (you're going to need it!). Acknowledge God's power.

🕴   And then we get to work on the story. Or rather, they get to work on it!

I am convinced that the more a group contributes to the creation and telling of a story, the more they get out of it and the more clearly they understand and appreciate it. So let's put them to work!

You'll need to split people up into five groups. Yes, I know there were six days of creation, but Days One and Two won't take as much 'illustrating' as the others, so we're giving that group two days to do. Let them break up into the groups that best suit them. If one group is much smaller than the rest, and some are much bigger, you might want to step in and do some reshuffling.

Send them to five 'art stations' that you will have set up previously around the room. If your room doesn't have that kind of space, or if you are limited by pews or other furniture, you can set up the stations in other rooms in the building. Only do this as a last resort, though. The hubbub of the creative process contained in one room adds to the general excitement and is reflective in some ways, I think, of the hubbub of creation. I'm a big one for hubbub.

You will want lots of art materials at the stations: big sheets of paper (those big rolls are great); big pieces of cloth; chunky markers; coloured paper; tape and glue and staplers. Go all out – we'll be using this stuff in some of our other stories too. Oh, and place a Bible and the relevant Bible reference (or a copy of the Bible passage) at each station and encourage each group to read the section they are illustrating before they begin.

What about those who say, 'I don't want to do it,' or, 'Art is not my thing'? Encourage them to join a group anyway to encourage and support the others. They might surprise themselves by coming up with an idea or two. It might also be helpful to say that 'art' won't be the main focus of every session and that there will be other kinds of activity down the line which they will find more appealing or comfortable. As a last resort (or perhaps a less strenuous alternative) you could get a group together to simply read the creation story out loud to each other.

So, what should each group create? Here are some suggestions, which you are free to give, but also give people the freedom to go in whatever direction works best for them.

Group One: Days One and Two (Genesis 1:3–8)

These need to be big pictures, because they form the foundation for the rest. So a big white banner or piece of paper for 'light' and a black one for 'dark'. Or they might want to dress or wrap someone up in white or black to represent that.

'Space', 'sky' and 'water' also need to be big, and there needs to be some sense of their relationship to each other: 'space' on top (no stars yet, please!), 'sky' in the middle, 'water' at the bottom.

Group Two: Day Three (Genesis 1:9–13)

Much easier, this one! You'll need something for 'earth' and 'sea' (wrapped-up people again?). And then lots of trees and flowers and shrubbery. Everyone could do an individual picture, or they could work together to build one big tree or plant. Or they could make one big plant out of all their little ones.

Group Three: Day Four (Genesis 1:14–19)

Sun, moon and stars. Pretty straightforward, really. Big pictures would do nicely, as would people with 'sun', 'moon' and 'star' hats or giant necklaces.

Group Four: Day Five (Genesis 1:20–23)

Sea creatures and birds. Again, they could draw pictures, make one big picture out of smaller ones, or they could make masks and 'play' the creatures themselves when the story is told.

Group Five: Day Six (Genesis 1:24–25)

Animals. Make sure there are some domesticated ones, some creepy-crawly ones and some wild ones. Use options as above.

How long should this take? I'd give your groups at least 15–20 minutes. But if as you circulate among them (that's your job, by the way: to encourage participation and answer questions and offer suggestions) you discover that the groups are finishing sooner than expected, then feel free to bring the activity to a close. I will often ask for a quick show of hands – 'Who needs more time?' – and then give a few more minutes if appropriate. If one group is really dragging its heels, however, I usually just get on with it and tell them (with a big smile – there's no need to be critical) to bring what they have finished.

Now you need a space, a pretty big space, where everyone can bring and show their work as the story is told. If your church has fixed pews, then that space will probably need to be at the front. If you have chairs that can be moved easily, you might want to clear a space in the middle, possibly before the service begins.

You might want some music as well. I know what church musicians are like. They tend to live on the 'cool' end of the personality spectrum (or at least that's where they'd like to live) and are therefore often disinclined to participate in group activities. If I'm being unfair here, I apologise, but that's my experience (and I was a worship leader for ten years). One way to draw them in to what's going on in the groups is to give them something 'musical' to do. Perhaps they can play something while the groups work. Nothing too loud, of course, but it's better than 'canned' music, I think. Or you could set them the task of coming up with a backing track for the story you're going to tell. If you feel more comfortable organising this with them earlier in the week, that's fine. I understand. But even then, they could practise that piece while the others are doing the art thing.

Right then, you're ready to tell the story at last. See the Story Box on pages 20–21.

How do you combine the art stuff with the story? As each day unfolds, you might want to start with a drumroll or a big noisy chord from the band (getting those musicians involved again). Then, as you say what happens each day, have the appropriate group bring their work forward to your performance space (front, centre, whatever). Have them stay there as you add the next bits on the next day and so forth, so that the 'display' gets bigger and bigger. At the end of each day, have everyone shout 'GOOD!' with you when you get to that part of the story. And as you tell it, make it just that bit faster and just that bit louder and just that bit more exciting as the story progresses. The background music will help this as well, if your band is playing along.

And then, at the end, when man and woman arrive at the climax of the story, have all the men and boys stand up and give a cheer followed by all the women and girls, who also give a cheer. After the final 'GOOD!', burst into songs of praise about God's creation, and give everyone the chance to celebrate the story. In fact, you might want whatever it is that the band is playing during the story to move directly into this 'praise' time – to make it all (seem) seamless and even more exciting.

Following the praise time, sit everyone down. They can either go back to their seats or, better still, sit down at the front or in the middle – wherever they were when the story finished. It's now time for just a little bit of teaching – teaching that will help your group to understand not only some of the implications of this story, but also all the stories to come. You can do this yourself, or, if you like, you can ask someone else to do it. Different voices are often an aid to concentration.

Ask this question: 'When God made the world, what was the most special thing he made?' You might get the right answer straight away, or it might take some time. If someone says 'armadillos', don't laugh (well, OK, you can chuckle a bit). Just say, 'Yeah, armadillos are amazing, but God made something even more special than that!'

Eventually (hopefully sooner rather than later) someone will say 'Adam and Eve' or 'people' or 'us'. And that's when you nod your head and point to that person, particularly if it's one of the children, and say, 'That's right. The most special thing God made when he made the world was you.' And then you point to some others as well and say, 'And you. And you. And you. And all of us. God made each of us special, like him, so we can love and communicate and create. But he made each of us different as well' (even twins, if someone should ask, and kids do!) – each with our own looks and gender and talents and shapes and colours.

'And in the garden, at the beginning, Adam and Eve, man and woman, were happy with who they were. Some people even say that's why they didn't mind being naked' (Yeah, giggles from the crowd here – no biggie). 'Because they weren't embarrassed about themselves. They were comfortable in their own skin. And that was GOOD.

'But that wasn't the only relationship that was good. Look at the person sitting next to you. Adam and Eve were comfortable with themselves and they were comfortable with each other as well. For, you see, God not only made you special and unique and precious, he made the person sitting next to you that way as well. If I'm the most special person in the universe, then I can get pretty selfish, but if you are as special as I am, then your needs are just as important as mine. And that's how God made us to love ourselves and each other. To see his image not just in me, but in the person sitting next to me too.

'Now look at the pictures we have drawn: the trees, the animals, the birds, the fishes.' (You might even want to ask a few to name their favourite bit of creation here.) 'All that God made for us, as an amazing and beautiful gift. In the garden, in the beginning, man's relationship was GOOD with his environment too. God asked us to take care of the world for him. To use it and to shape it and to follow his example in making more beauty from it. Not to destroy it and abuse it. That's why God asked Adam to name the animals: so that there would be a close and personal and loving relationship with the world.

'And finally, there was one more GOOD relationship in the beginning, and that was between man and God. They talked together, freely and openly. There was nothing to hide. So we're going to talk to God now, and give him thanks for all he made for us, and ask for his help as we live in his beautiful world.'

🌰 I'd do 'open eye' prayers here. Have everyone look at their hands and give thanks for themselves and maybe ask God to help them appreciate what an amazing person he made when he made them.

I'd have them look at each other next and give thanks for the person next to them, and ask for his help in treating others as though they were special.

Have them look at the drawings, etc. next and give thanks for the world and all that's in it. Then ask for wisdom in using and taking care of that world.

Finally, have everyone thank God himself for his love and power, and ask his help in keeping in touch with him and talking with him.

🎵   And then one last song, with everyone standing. Tell them that on Day Seven God rested, and now it's time for them to go home and do that too. And you're done!

Note: If you have made a large tree as part of the activity time, you may wish to keep it for Story 2 and/or 3.

SCRIPT

 Explain your noise management control system for the story time

As it happens, however, I don't want to start with the story. I want to start with God. Because that's where the story starts: God, just God, Father, Son and Spirit, before anything was made.

 God's creative power and majesty

 Acknowledging God's power

 Days of creation

 Creation (Genesis 1)

Day One – God said, 'Light!' And there it was, just like that. Not sunlight. Not starlight. But pure light. Bright and white like an empty canvas. He set the light on one side and called it day. And he set the darkness on the other and called it night. And there was morning and there was evening and it was GOOD!

Day Two – God said, 'Sky!' And there it was, just like that. And it was bright and it was blue and it was thundery and it was grey. And above it there was space and below it there was water. And there was morning and there was evening and it was GOOD!

Day Three – God said, 'Earth!' And there it was, just like that. And the waters parted before it and there was land and there was sea. And then grass sprouted and trees grew and flowers blossomed. And there was morning and there was evening and it was GOOD!

Day Four – God said, 'Sun!' and there it was, just like that. Big and bright and blazing. Then God said, 'Moon!' as well. And, 'Stars!' for good measure. And the blackness of space was sprinkled with light, and blinked and sparkled and shone. And there was morning and there was evening and it was GOOD!

Day Five – God said, 'Fish!' And there they were, just like that. And the rivers shook and the seas swelled with their leaping and swimming and splashing. Then God said, 'Birds!' and they burst from the clouds and their cries filled the skies. And there was morning and there was evening and it was GOOD!

Day Six – God said, 'Animals!' And there they were, just like that. Hoofs hammered and manes shook and trunks trumpeted. And there was morning and there was evening and it was GOOD!

But it was not yet good enough. There was something missing. Well, some ONE, actually. Someone to enjoy all this goodness. Someone to take care of it and treasure it and write songs about it. Someone to thank God for it.

So God spoke again. And what he said was, 'People!' And there they were, just like that. And there they were, just like us. Man *(men and boys stand and cheer)* and woman *(women and girls stand and cheer)*. Me and you.

And there was morning and there was evening and it was GOOD!

Alternative story-tellings:

Simply read the passage straight from Genesis chapter 1! But practise it – read it well!

C. S. Lewis's retelling of creation in The Magician's Nephew *is an absolute classic. If read well with music in the background, it might be a nice start to the whole service. There's an audio version with Kenneth Branagh reading that would be amazing!*

Steve Turner has done a poetic retelling of the creation story, which is lovely and amazing in its simplicity. It is also available in his volume of poetry, The Day I Fell Down the Toilet.

I have also written other creation retellings, which you might find useful. There is one at the beginning of The Lion Storyteller Bible, *and one focused more on Adam and the naming of the animals in my book* Telling the Bible.

I have also written a creation song called 'God Made Me', which you might find helpful. It's on the Spring Harvest Pre-School Praise 1 *CD.*

Praise for God's creation

 God created us to have a good relationship with him

When God made the world, what was the most special thing he made? *(Adam and Eve or people or us)*

That's right, the most special thing God made when he made the world was you. And you. And you. And you. And all of us.

God made each of us special, like him, so we can love and communicate and create. But he made each of us different as well – each with our own looks and gender and talents and shapes and colours.

And in the garden, at the beginning, Adam and Eve, man and woman, were happy with who they were. Some people even say that's why they didn't mind being naked. Because they weren't embarrassed about themselves. They were comfortable in their own skin. And that was GOOD!

But that wasn't the only relationship that was good. Look at the person sitting next to you. Adam and Eve were comfortable with themselves, and they were comfortable with each other as well. For, you see, God not only made you special and unique and precious, he made the person sitting next to you that way as well. If I'm the most special person in the universe, then I can get pretty selfish, but if you are as special as I am, then your needs are just as important as mine. And that's how God made us to love ourselves and each other. To see his image not just in me, but in the person sitting next to me too.

Now look at the pictures we have drawn: the trees, the animals, the birds, the fishes. All that God made for us, as an amazing and beautiful gift. In the garden, in the beginning, man's relationship was GOOD with his environment too. God asked us to take care of the world for him. To use it and to shape it and to follow his example in making more beauty from it. Not to destroy it and abuse it. That's why God asked Adam to name the animals: so that there would be a close and personal and loving relationship with the world.

And finally, there was one more GOOD relationship in the beginning, and that was between man and God. They talked together, freely and openly. There was nothing to hide. So we're going to talk to God now, and give him thanks for all he made for us, and ask for his help as we live in his beautiful world.

 Thanks to God

 Praise for God's creation

On Day Seven God rested, and now it's time for you to go home and do that too.

All-Age Services

STORY 2

THE FALL

In advance

Prepare trees, fruit-shaped paper, volunteers to wear the right coloured clothes; rehearse Adam, Eve and serpent if appropriate.

Christmas tree ornaments, including one with a nativity theme; a cross; animal puppet or stuffed toy (preferably a platypus!); holly branch; pair of jeans.

Outline

1st Start with God

Thanking God for his willingness to have a loving relationship with us

God's love for us and the world he created

Tree dressing

The Fall (Genesis 2–3)

Praise for God's creation

Good turned to bad. We need to be brought back into a good relationship with God. . .

Sorry for turning God's good fruit into bad

Sorry

. . .and God promises that will happen

Jesus died to bring us back to God

1st   We need to start with trees. Well, two trees: the Tree of Life and the Tree of the Knowledge of Good and Evil.

If you made a tree in the creation story (assuming you did the creation story before this one, and if not, why not?), then you can use that for the Tree of Life. If you don't have a tree from the previous story, then I suggest you use an artificial Christmas tree for the Tree of Life, covered with lights and ornaments, and you can use that later when we talk about God's coming promise in Story 7. Excellent!

The Tree of the Knowledge of Good and Evil is a little trickier. You could make a tree out of cardboard or mesh or wood, but I think it would be much more interesting to make it out of people. You'll need volunteers, five or six for each side, but don't worry if you can't get that many or want to use more. Ask half of them to dress all in black, or in dark colours at the very least (even down to black gloves if you can find enough). Have the other side dress all in white, or light and bright colours. The contrast is the key thing. Masks might also be interesting. They don't have to be complicated, just simple face shapes that look sad or glad or angry or happy or peaceful or hateful – again to make a contrast.

Stand the volunteers on several different levels (floor, step, chair, ladder – that kind of thing), two bodies wide, standing behind each other, so the bodies look like part of the trunk, and the arms (reaching up high or out to one side) look like the branches. You can either build the tree so one whole side is light and the other dark, or you can mix them up – the colours will show the difference. The tree will need to be standing there, beside the Tree of Life, right from the start of the service. Just have them stand straight with their arms to their sides at the start, otherwise their arms will get really tired, and then have them 'open their branches' when you tell the story.

And that's where we start our service.

Say something like: 'God made the world. He made it good. And then he planted a garden in the east, in a place called Eden. It was a beautiful garden, a perfect garden. And Adam and Eve called it home. They talked with God. And they walked with God. They knew every animal by name. They lived naked, without fear or shame. And life was perfect, just perfect.'

Now would be a good time for the group to talk with God as well. Lead them in a prayer that thanks God for the world and for his desire to walk and talk with us; to live in a loving relationship with us.

Sing a song (or two or three) that celebrates the world God made and his love for us. Focus as much on the relationship as on creation. The one is a result of the other.

Something you might like to try as a part of this block of songs is the Bob Dylan tune 'Man gave names to all the animals', which is on his album *Slow Train Coming*. The melody is pretty simple, once you have listened closely enough to pick it out, and the chorus is easy to learn. When I did it, I taught the group the chorus and sang the verse myself, giving the kids a chance to guess the animal in each verse. You could even flash some fun pictures of those animals up on the screen when they guess it. It's a great song, and once your band has finished with all their bad Dylan impersonations, you'll all have fun with it.

Now back to the story. Tell them that God planted all kinds of trees in the garden. Trees that were good to look at. Trees that were good to eat from. And then he planted two very special trees in the middle of the garden: the Tree of Life (you point to the appropriate tree) and the Tree of the Knowledge of Good and Evil (this is where they spread their arm-branches). We don't know what either of them looked like, so we're going to have to use our imagination a bit as we bring them to life.

Give everyone a couple of things to do. Pass out paper cut into the shape of fruit. Nothing too big, and feel free to use any fruit shape you like. Oranges are probably easiest to cut out, but bananas are a close second, I think, and pineapples a distant eighth or ninth! And, yes, you can use apples if you must (and are keen to perpetuate a common misunderstanding!). Actually, a mix of fruits might be best, seeing as we have no idea of what the fruit on that tree really was. You might even be able to find notepaper already cut into the shape of fruit at a stationers or card shop. Hey, take the easy way out is what I say! Once everyone has two shapes, have them write a 'good' thing (behaviour, attitude, etc.) on one fruit, and a 'bad' thing on another. Folk will have to help the really little ones, but this is an all-age activity, after all. Then ask people to take the fruit shapes to the Tree of the Knowledge of Good and Evil and put the 'good' fruit in the hands of the 'good' branches and the 'bad' fruit into the hands of the 'bad' branches. See why we used people for this tree?

Then, if you're using a Christmas tree for the Tree of Life (and the more I think about it, the more perfect I think that is), let everyone help decorate it at this point. Have a box of Christmas ornaments (the less fragile kind would be preferable) by the side of the tree, and have a couple of volunteers hand the ornaments out and help people to hang the ornaments on the tree if necessary.

Once everyone is sitting down again, find yourself an Adam and Eve. You need to find folk who are happy to stand at the front and act out their parts with gusto. They can be children or adults – it doesn't matter, just as long as they're willing to play along. Of course, you can choose these people ahead of time if you like, and run over the script with them in the week before. It's totally up to you.

Parts? Scripts? That's right, we're going to do a little drama-type thing now, but with some story-telling-type participation woven in. Adam and Eve are there simply to lead the men/boys and women/girls in saying the Adam and Eve lines. You will need to explain this to everyone, and perhaps even practise one or two of the lines from the script to give them an idea of how it works. It's simple really: you say the line, then Adam or Eve leads his or her respective group in saying it after you. And speaking of you – you get to be the serpent! All right, if you don't feel up to it or aren't keen, you can find someone to act the part out and even dress up if they like (I'd go for a really expensive suit if it were me, something stylish and sophisticated) while you narrate. But it's probably easier, and cleaner, for you to tell the story and do the serpent lines, just because there are so many. It won't hurt if you're working from a script – people will expect that – but if your serpent actor has a piece of paper in front of his face, it will look messy. If, on the other hand, you do have someone who can act, and doesn't mind memorising lines, then by all means rope them in. Oh, and in spite of what I said above about the suit, you could have a lady serpent if you like.

Right then, back to the story. The script is in the Story Box on pages 27–29.

? At this point someone needs to do a little teaching, and since the group has been listening to you for quite a long time now, perhaps that someone needs to be someone else. The teaching is simple really, and it connects directly to what your group learned in the creation story. Having said that, there is enough information about creation spelled out in the teaching, so if you didn't do that prior to this one, your group will still understand the point. The teaching script is on pages 29–30.

♪ We're going to pray now and we're going to use our Tree of Knowledge to help us. Take some of the 'bad fruit' and read them out – three or four at a time. Then say together, 'We are sorry, God, for turning your good gifts into something bad.' Use as many slips of paper as appropriate – try to mix things up a bit. You might even want to have the people who make up the tree do the reading out loud, taking turns from branch to branch. Perhaps they could quietly and unobtrusively sort through the papers ahead of time, while you are speaking.

♪ Explain that you are going to sing a song together, telling God how sorry we are.

? Conclude with the second part of the teaching script.

♪ Finally, sing a song or two about what Jesus did to bring us back to God. And you are finished!

SCRIPT

1st   God made the world. He made it good. And then he planted a garden in the east, in a place called Eden. It was a beautiful garden, a perfect garden. And Adam and Eve called it home. They talked with God. And they walked with God. They knew every animal by name. They lived naked, without fear or shame. And life was perfect, just perfect.

Now would be a good time for us to talk with God as well.

 Thanking God for his willingness to have a loving relationship with us

 God's love for us and the world he created

 Tree dressing

God planted all kinds of trees in the garden. Trees that were good to look at. Trees that were good to eat from. And then he planted two very special trees in the middle of the garden: the Tree of Life and the Tree of the Knowledge of Good and Evil (*this is where they spread their arm-branches*). We don't know what either of them looked like, so we're going to have to use our imagination a bit as we bring them to life.

 The Fall (Genesis 2–3)

Of all the creatures that God made, the serpent was by far the most clever. 'Tell me,' he said to Eve one day, 'did God really say that you are not allowed to eat from any of the trees in the garden?'

Eve shook her head. *(Your Eve leads all the females in shaking their heads)*

And then she said, 'We can eat from any tree.' *(Eve and all the females repeat this line)*

'Except for the tree in the middle of the garden.' *(Eves repeat)*

'If we eat from that one, we will die.' *(Eves repeat)*

The serpent laughed. And it was not a nice laugh. 'You won't die!' he sneered. 'If you eat from that tree *(point to the Knowledge Tree)*, then you will know what God knows – evil as well as good. And if you know what he knows, then you will be just like him!'

Eve looked at the fruit and rubbed her belly. *(Eves rub bellies)* She was hungry.

Eve looked at the fruit and licked her lips. *(Eves lick lips)* It smelled delicious.

'This will make me as wise as God,' she thought.

And so she picked a piece. *(Eve up front takes a fruit-shaped piece of paper from the tree)*

And she took a great big juicy bite. *(Eves pretend to bite)*

Then she called out, 'Adam!' *(Eves repeat, hand to mouth, calling motion)*

And Adam said, 'Huh?' *(Adams repeat, just ever so slightly slack-jawed)*

He was preoccupied, trying to figure out what to name the platypus. Furry Flat Face? Ducky Billed Mammal-Like Egg-dropping thing? It was hard work, and he had already discovered that he was no good at doing two things at once! *(Might be fun to have him holding a platypus puppet or stuffed animal)*

'Adam!' said Eve again. *(Eves repeat)*

'Taste this fruit.' *(Eves repeat)*

'It will make you as wise as God!' *(Eves repeat)*

'As wise as God?' thought Adam. 'That could be quite handy when it comes to naming platypuses – hey, that's a good name for the duck-billed thing!' *(No need to repeat this, as it's a thought, but if your Adam and Eve practise ahead of time, Adam could stand there in a thinking pose)*

So Adam took the fruit. *(Adam up front takes fruit-shaped paper)*

And Adam took a bite. *(Adams all take a bite)*

And as soon he did, he knew something all right. Adam knew that he was naked.

'Aaaah! I'm naked!' *(Adams repeat, and if he is holding a platypus, he could use it to quickly cover up his nether regions)*

And Eve shrieked, 'Aaah! I'm naked too!' *(Eves repeat)*

And they sewed leaves together to cover themselves.

(The following gag will only work if you choose your Adam and Eve ahead of time, but you could have them scramble about, around and behind the trees, and have Adam emerge with some kind of prickly holly branch, grimacing. Then have Eve emerge holding a pair of jeans. Adam looks at Eve, puzzled. 'What's that?'

'A little something I put together,' *she answers, looking at the tag.* 'They're Leaf-is!' *(Expect massive groans)*

Later that day, Adam and Eve heard God walking through the garden, so they hid *(behind Tree of Life would probably work best)*.

'Where are you?' God called. *(Again, I think it's just easier if you play the part of God, but if you have someone off-stage or in the sound booth doing the God voice, try very hard to avoid the 'massive reverb' thing. I think it sends the wrong message and works against the sense of sorrow and disappointment we want to hear in God's voice at this point.)*

And Adam called back. 'I'm naked.' *(Adams repeat)*

'I'm afraid.' *(Adams repeat)*

'I'm hiding.' *(Adams repeat)*

'Who told you you were naked?' asked God. And then God gasped. And then God sighed, 'You've eaten from the Knowledge Tree, haven't you?'

And Adam pointed at Eve and said, 'It was her fault!' *(Adams repeat)*

'She gave me the fruit!' *(Adams repeat)*

So God turned to Eve. 'Is that what you did?' he asked.

And Eve pointed at the serpent. 'It was his fault.' *(Eves repeat)*

'He tricked me!' *(Eves repeat)*

So God turned to the serpent and said, 'Because you have done this, you are cursed. You will crawl on your belly. You will choke on the dust. And this woman and her children will be your enemies. You will bite their heels, but they will crush your head.'

Then he turned to Eve. 'Because you have done this, you will have great pain in child-bearing, and your husband will rule over you.'

And finally, God said to Adam, 'Because you have done this, the ground will be hard and your work will too. You will struggle to bring food from the earth. And when your life is over, you will return to the dust from which you came.'

Everyone was sad. God most of all. So he sent Adam and Eve out of the garden, and put an angel with a flaming sword at the entrance, so they could never return. *(Adam and Eve walk sadly away)*

 Praise for God's creation

 Good turned to bad. We need to be brought back into a good relationship with God. . .

When God made the world, he made it good. Good in lots of ways. But when Adam and Eve ate from the Tree of the Knowledge of Good and Evil, they turned those good things bad. God made us to be happy with ourselves – to appreciate our uniqueness and our talents. One of the ways the Bible expresses that is when it talks about Adam and Eve walking naked in the garden. They were happy with themselves; there was nothing to be afraid or ashamed of. But when they ate the fruit, they tried to cover themselves – they were no longer happy as they were.

They were no longer happy with each other either. When God made the world, he made the relationship between people good as well. But when Adam and Eve ate the fruit, they blamed each other and stopped trusting each other.

And there is more. When God made the world, he gave it as a gift to Adam and Eve. It was theirs to care for and watch over and enjoy. Things were good between them and the world. But after they ate the fruit, Adam had to work hard to get any food from the ground.

Finally, when God made the world, he made things good between him and man and woman. They talked with him. They looked forward to being with him. But after they ate the fruit, they wanted to hide from him. Things turned bad there as well.

And the saddest thing is that all those good-turned-bad things are still with us. We still don't always like or respect ourselves the way God made us. We still treat other people badly, failing to see the beautiful acts of creation that they are. We still abuse the world instead of taking care of it. And we still need to be brought back into a good relationship with God.

 Sorry for turning God's good fruit into bad

 Sorry

 . . . and God promises that will happen

This is a sad story, isn't it? God gave Adam and Eve so many wonderful things, but they messed up, they sinned, and everything around them got messed up too.

But that didn't stop God from loving them, just like he never stops loving us when we do things that are wrong.

He made a promise in this story. A promise to make things good again. A promise you might have missed because it popped up in the most unexpected place.

Do you remember what God said to the serpent? He told the serpent that he would bite the heel of the woman's child, and that the child would crush his head.

Christians believe that was a promise – a prophecy of something that would one day happen. Adam and Eve didn't know when, but we do! And it's right here, in the Tree of Life. We don't know what the Tree of Life really looked like, and you may have been wondering why we made it a Christmas tree. *(Reach for an ornament with a nativity theme at this point)* We did that because the child who was promised way back when the world began came to us at Christmas time. He was Jesus! *(Now reach round the back of the tree, where you will have hung a wooden cross at the start)* And while the serpent did wound him on the cross *(show it)*, his death made things good for ever between us and God again, and crushed that serpent's head. So maybe this *(point to Christmas tree)* isn't the Tree of Life at all. *(Hold up the cross for all to see)* Maybe it looks like this!

   Jesus died to bring us back to God

ABRAHAM

In advance

Prepare tree, green paper leaves, copies of story song lyrics.

Outline

- Promise leaves
- God's faithfulness and trustworthiness
- Thanking God for keeping his promises
- Part 1: Abraham (Genesis 12:1–9)
- Story songs (Genesis 12:10–20; 13:1–18; 16:1–4)
- Part 2: Abraham (Genesis 17:1 – 18:15; 21:1–7)
- God keeps his promises
- Thank God for all his promises
- Laugh poem
- God is faithful

OK, we start with one more tree. But this is the last one, I promise! And speaking of promises, that's where our story starts as well. So before you do anything else, have everyone get into pairs – older people with younger people where possible – and have them write down something that someone promised them, or that they promised someone else. Encourage them to come up with their most interesting 'promise' stories and have them write those promises down on a leaf. Green paper leaves are probably the easiest – make them whatever size you like. But if you want to use something fancier, such as green foil or green wrapping paper, make sure you give everyone something to write with that will show up on the leaf. Now ask a few volunteers to share their promises/promise stories with everyone, and when they have done so, have them come up and stick their leaves onto a paper tree that you have at the front (blu-tack works great). You could use your tree from Story 1, or make one out of stiff cardboard, so it stands up on its own, or have a large picture of a tree fixed to a wall – I'll leave (sorry) that to you! But it needs to be big enough so that you can sit under it to tell your story later on.

When a few have spoken, invite everyone else to stick their promise-leaves onto the tree as well (get the musicians to play while they do this).

As the last people make their way back to their seats, launch into a block of songs that focus on God's faithfulness and trustworthiness.

After the singing, lead them in a prayer that gives thanks to God for keeping his promises. If appropriate, you might want to refer to some of the promise stories people have already heard.

When you have finished the prayer, tell your group that God makes promises and that he is very good at keeping them. If you have done the story of the Fall before this one, you might even ask them if they remember the promise God made in that story.

If not, simply tell them that God made the world good. That people turned it bad when they disobeyed God – when they sinned. And that even though God was sad and disappointed, he still loved them and had a plan to put things right. He promised that one day a child of Eve would win the battle over evil – crush the serpent's head – and make things good again. To do that, God needed to make a family from which that child could come. And that family is the family that they will be meeting today: the family of a man called Abram. Which works very nicely, actually, because the name Abram means 'father'.

God promised Abram a big family – a really big family. So big, in fact, that he compared it to 'the stars in the sky' and 'the sand on the seashore'.

Tell your group that we'll be using those phrases several times, so this is what we'll do when we hear them. Divide the group into two – just splitting the room in half will be the easiest thing. Have one half stand up, wiggle their fingers and say 'twinkle, twinkle, twinkle!' in high, squeaky little voices whenever they hear the phrase 'the stars in the sky'. Have the other half stand up, do a hula move and say 'shifty, shifty, shifty!' (for the shifting sands – get it?) whenever they hear the phrase 'the sand on the seashore'.

Tell them, as well, that God's promise to Abram was a kind of funny promise (both 'funny strange' and 'funny ha-ha'), because when God made his promise to Abram, Abram was already 75 years old. His wife Sarah wasn't much younger, and they had no children at all! So whenever anyone in the story finds God's promise funny, you will lead the group in a little 'laughing' exercise. Divide them into three groups (perhaps front, middle and back of the room this time). Have the first group give a little giggle, which will grow into a chuckle with the second group, and then into a belly laugh with the third group. Practise this with them a time or two before you start the story, pointing to each group in turn (like a laugh-conductor!) so they get it just right.

Now you can start the story, but don't sit under the tree just yet. The rest of the story is in the Story Box on page XX.

And now for a brief musical interlude. Several things happen to Abram between his 'calling' and the event that is at the heart of this service. Each of these incidents demonstrates something about God's watchful care over Abram and Sarah and the promise he made to them. So I thought it would be fun to do little musical versions of those stories. Divide into the three groups you put everyone in for the 'laughing' activity. Send them to three different parts or stations of the room, where you will have already placed either (a) individual slips of paper with the song lyrics on (hopefully having guesstimated enough for everyone in each group) or (b) one large poster-sized piece of paper with the lyrics on that someone can hold in front of the group while they sing.

Tunes? The tune for all the groups will be the same. Because Abram's descendants will be more numerous than the stars in the sky, the songs will all be sung to the tune of 'Twinkle, twinkle, little star'!

Put a Bible at each station as well, and have someone from each group read the story to the rest of their group. Then ask the groups to practise their song and maybe come up with some simple song actions that everyone can do, or perhaps they could 'act' the song out or, if you want to include an art activity, they could draw an illustration relating to the song – although that would take you a lot more time and require a lot more materials. Still, you know your group, so do what suits them.

Once everyone has practised, sit the whole group back down again and sing the stories in this order:

1. Genesis 12:10–20

Abram's wife was old but pretty,
So when a famine sent them to Egypt city
Abram pretended she was his sister.
Pharaoh said, 'I quite fancy her, mister!'
God made Pharaoh sick as a dog and
Abram and Sarah escaped to their own land.

2. Genesis 13:1–18

Abram's nephew Lot was greedy.
He didn't want land that was hard and weedy,
So Abram gave him the lion's share
And took whatever plots were spare.
They burst forth with fauna and flora
While Lot moved next to Sodom and Gomorrah.

3. Genesis 16:1–4

Abram grew real tired of waitin'.
He had a child with Sarah's maiden.
Ishmael was his firstborn son
But God said, 'No, he's not the one.
The promise is for Sarah and you.
Just be patient, it will all come true.'

Once the songs are finished continue with the story from the Story Box.

Now have everyone get together with their original partners (the ones they told the promises to) and very quickly have them tell their partner a promise that God or Jesus makes in the Bible. Then ask for volunteers to share their Bible promise so they can see that God made promises not only to Abram. Go on to ask people to tell of promises that God has made to them personally. You can say a bit about how he makes those promises come true.

Lead everyone in a prayer thanking God for all his promises.

Read the poem 'Laugh'.

Finish with some more upbeat God-is-faithful songs.
  The end!

SCRIPT

 Promise leaves

 God's faithfulness and trustworthiness

 Thanking God for keeping his promises

Part 1: Abraham (Genesis 12:1–9)

One day, God spoke to a man named Abram. Why he chose Abram, no one knows. It was a gift – an amazing gift that would change Abram and the world for ever.

'I want to make you the father of a very special family. A nation, in fact,' God told Abram. 'You will have more children than there are stars in the sky *(twinkle action)*, more children than there are grains of sand on the seashore *(shifty action)* and this family will one day bless the whole world.'

Abram was amazed at God's offer, but he couldn't help having a little laugh *(laugh actions)*. He was 75 years old. His wife Sarah wasn't much younger, and well past child-bearing age. 'How will God manage this?' he wondered. But Abram trusted God – that was the key thing. So even though God's offer seemed impossible, Abram took it.

'What do you want me do?' he asked.

'Pack up your things,' God said. 'Your tents and your animals and all you have. And follow me. I have a special place I want to take you. And a special land I want to give you. That's my promise.'

So Abram did what God asked. He packed his things, and saddled up his beasts, and gathered his relatives, and he left his home and followed God to the land of Canaan.

 Story songs (Genesis 12:10–20; 13:1–18; 16:1–4)

 Part 2: Abraham (Genesis 17:1 – 18:15; 21:1–7)

God watched over Abram and Sarah to make sure his promise would come true. He saved them from Pharaoh, he gave them the best land, away from the evil towns of Sodom and Gomorrah, and even though Abram tried to make the promise come true in his own way, God did not give up on him.

But a lot of time passed. And by the time we meet Abram again he is 99 years old and the promise seems more impossible than ever. Nothing has changed. He has no son by Sarah. And to make matters worse, God has given him a new name, Abraham, which doesn't just mean 'father'; it means 'father of many nations'!

(Now sit down under the promise tree) Abraham sat under a tree, the great tree of Mamre. There was his tent. His old wife was working inside. There was the sun, beating down on him in the middle of the day. But all Abraham could think about was God's promise: I will make a great nation of you. Your children will be more numerous than the stars in the sky *(action)* or the sands on the seashore *(action)*. Twenty-five long years had passed since God made that promise and, truth to tell, Abraham had just about given up on it.

And then something happened. Three men came walking by, and all he knew was they had something of God about them. They might have been very holy men. They might have been angels. They might somehow have been God himself.

Abraham bowed before them and then offered to wash their feet and bring them something to eat. They accepted his hospitality, and while they waited, Abraham hurried off to Sarah in the tent and asked her to bake some bread. Then he hurried to his herd of cows and picked a calf and asked a servant to kill it and cook it. Then he hurried back to his guests and served them the meal. Abraham was nearly a hundred years old. Hurrying was hard.

But as they ate, they asked him a question: 'Where is Sarah, your wife?'

'In the tent,' Abraham huffed and puffed.

'We will come back next year,' said the guests. 'And by that time Sarah will have a son.' Now Sarah was still in the tent. But she wasn't at the back. No, she was right up front, sitting at the entrance. Listening!

And when she heard what the guests had to say, she couldn't believe it. 'I'm too old,' she thought. 'Too old to have a child. Too old for that kind of joy.' And then she giggled *(action)*. And then she chuckled *(action)*. And then she laughed right out loud *(action)* at the thought of it. So loud, in fact, that the guests heard her.

'Sarah is laughing!' they said. 'Does she not know that there is nothing too hard for God? Trust us – when we come back next year she will indeed have a child.'

And so she did. Sarah. Old Sarah. Sarah well beyond child-bearing age gave birth to a son. And when she did, she called him Isaac, which means 'laughter'. *(Do the three laughter actions as a kind of finale)*

Storytelling options:

You can simply tell the story straight from the Scriptures if you like. As you have seen, I have stayed pretty close to the text.

There is also a very nice retelling of the Abraham story in my book The Lion Storyteller Bible.

 *God keeps his promises*

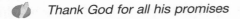 *Thank God for all his promises*

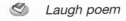 *Laugh poem*

When I think that God made kangaroos

With pockets on their bellies

And wrink-e-ly rhin-o-cer-i

And fish that look like jellies

The puffin and the pangolin

The gnu and the giraffe

Then I just gotta laugh.

Yeah, I just gotta laugh.

And Abraham laughed

And Sarah laughed

And God laughed up his sleeve

To think that these two pensioners

Would need maternity leave.

And Sarah laughed

And Abraham laughed

And when the baby came

They called their newborn Isaac
And 'laughter' was his name.

When I think that God made elephants
With trunks in place of noses
And bitey Venus Fly Trap plants
With teeth instead of roses
And what about the platypus?
Bird? Mammal? Half and half?
Well, I just gotta laugh.
Yeah, I just gotta laugh.

And Abraham laughed
And Sarah laughed
And God went crazy-happy
To think that these two pensioners
Would soon be changing nappies.
And Sarah laughed
And Abraham laughed
And when the baby came
They called their newborn Isaac
And 'laughter' was his name.

 God is faithful

EXODUS

In advance

Prepare visual presentation for the story: Ten Commandment tablets.

Outline

1st God's children in slavery (Exodus 1)

🎵 God's help in times of trouble

🔥 Help us, Lord

📖 Part 1: Exodus (Exodus 5–15)

🎵 God saves us and sets us free

📖 Part 2: Exodus (Exodus 19)

🏃 Ten Commandments

📖 Part 3: Exodus (Exodus 20)

❓ Foretelling freedom through Jesus, or present-day slavery

🎵 Thank God for setting us free

1st   You know those paper chains? The ones you make by interlocking strips of paper into links? Well, that's what I'd like you to start this service with.

You can either make them ahead of time (four links each should be sufficient, with the ends big enough to slip a hand through), or you can have your group make them as their first activity when they come into the room. As usual, have several stations for doing this set up around the room so that everyone doesn't get jammed up at one table. Once everyone has their chains fitted on their wrists, tell them to sit down.

Then start the service by giving them a very short history lesson. Say something like: 'Abraham (whom we met last time) had a son named Isaac – remember?' And you might even see if anyone remembers what his name meant. 'Isaac had two sons, Jacob and Esau, who didn't get along very well. There was nothing to laugh about there. God changed Jacob's name to Israel, and he had twelve sons. The most famous of them all was Joseph, who went to Egypt and with God's help saved both the Egyptians and his own family from starvation. And there the children of Israel multiplied, until there were loads and loads and loads of them.'

If you'd like to, and have someone talented at this, you could illustrate this bit on a screen. A simple PowerPoint of an ever-expanding family (One – One – Two – Twelve – then a multitude – that sort of thing. Even simple stick figures will do, if they're fun). Or you could take photos of people from your church dressed up in robes and beards, and do the family tree that way. Or maybe even grab pics off the net: old-fashioned drawings of the patriarchs (maybe even with funny bubble thoughts pasted in); a YouTube clip from *Joseph and the Amazing Technicolor Dreamcoat*. I'm sure you have some mischievous computer types who would love to do something a little irreverent here! Just be sure you check it out ahead of time, in case the irreverence gets the better of them.

'The Bible says that one day a man came to rule Egypt, a pharaoh, who did not remember what Joseph had done for his people. He was worried about the children of Israel – worried that there were so many of them. So he turned them into his slaves and set them to work, building his great cities.

'That's why we're wearing these chains on our wrists: to remind us that they were slaves and could not escape.

'But there are different kinds of slavery, aren't there? Can anyone raise their hand and tell me?' (Hopefully someone tries to raise a hand.) 'See, you can't do it, can you? The chains mean you have to raise both hands – you can't do what you want to do. You're under somebody or something else's control.'

And then you might want to mention the different kinds of slavery, or take more answers from the group. These might include sin, bad habits, addictions, and someone might even mention modern forms of slavery.

'When the children of Israel were enslaved, they cried out to God, and that's how we will start our time together.'

🎵   Sing a sad and quiet song or two that deals with our need for God's help in times of trouble.

🔥   Then lead everyone in a 'Help us, Lord' kind of prayer. You might like to lead them in a reading of the first two verses of Psalm 88. Or have them repeat it after you, line by line.

📖   Now go back to your illustrated history lesson (plenty of Charlton Heston clips available for your computer people here). Use the Story Box on pages 46–47.

'God heard his people's cry for freedom, and he sent a man named Moses to lead them out of slavery. With God's help, Moses fought with Pharaoh, bringing plague after plague on the people of Egypt. Hail and gnats and frogs and more – ten plagues altogether. And then, after the final plague, when the firstborn children of Egypt died, Pharaoh let the people of Israel go. Or so it seemed. For at the last moment Pharaoh changed his mind and sent his army to bring them back. The people of Israel were trapped. The Egyptian army was behind them and the Red Sea was in front of them. All hope was lost. And then in one final mighty act of freedom, God told Moses to lift his staff. The waters of the Red Sea parted and the children of Israel walked through. But when Pharaoh's army tried to follow, the waters crashed down around them and they drowned. The children of Israel were free!

'So stand up and lift your hands in the air, and on the count of ten – for those ten plagues – I want you to tear off your chains. Are you ready? One, two, three, four, five, six, seven, eight, nine, ten. TEAR OFF YOUR CHAINS!'

🎵   And as soon as they do, have your band prepped to burst immediately into a song of celebration about how God saves us and sets us free. Sing one or two more after that. Really celebrate.

Here's a nice alternative for you to consider: Prior to the tearing of the chains, you might like to tell everyone that once the people had crossed the sea and Pharaoh's army had been drowned, they sang a song of praise to God. I absolutely love this psalm (Exodus 15:1–13) and if you have someone who can read it really well, to bring out its power and imagery, or if you have a dance group that could interpret it while it is being read, that would be really effective. Then you could tear the chains and invite your group to sing as well.

📖   Now carry on with the story in the Story Box.

'So God set his people free. But he wanted them to stay free as well, and he wanted to remind them that they were his people, descendants of their father, Abraham, whom he'd called to follow him all those years ago, and the people through whom he intended to bless the world. Remember? That's the promise he'd made to Abraham. All part of the promise he'd made to Adam and Eve. And God keeps his promises.

'So just as he sent ten plagues to set them free, he gave them ten rules to keep them free – and to keep them close to him. We call them the Ten Commandments, and we're going to have a look at them now.'

Divide your group into ten smaller groups and send them to ten stations set at even intervals around the room. Start with number one at the front, just left of centre (as you're looking from the front), and move clockwise around the room. Yeah, I'm confused too. There will be a cardboard tablet (you know – the kind of thing Charlton Heston carried down the hill: the rounded-top tombstone-shaped thing!) at each station, and on the tablet will be the number of the commandment and a short modern description. Tell them that they are to read that description and then come up with a tableau, a frozen moment, to depict that commandment for the others when it is their turn. I have included some suggestions, which you can put on the tablet as well, but encourage them to use their own imaginations.

When they have finished, read the following, but lead everyone in the counting exercise before each commandment, and let someone in each group read the commandment out loud while the others make the tableau.

Oh, and tell them all to make the thunder and lightning sounds with you *(Crash! Flash!)* and to blow trumpets *(Toot!)* when they blast. Might need a quick practice.

Three months after God's people left Egypt, they came to a mountain called Sinai.

Thunder crashed! Lightning flashed! And with a trumpet blast God came down upon the mountain in a cloud of fire and smoke.

The mountain trembled, like a volcano about to burst.

And God's people trembled too.

Then God called to Moses from the cloud, and Moses climbed the mountain to meet him. 'I want you to talk to my people,' God said. 'My people, whom I rescued from the land of Egypt. The whole world is mine, but they are my special people. A people for all the world to see. A people through whom I will bless the world. And if they are to be my special people, then this is how they must live:

One. . .

There is only one God. That's me. And you mustn't give your hearts to anyone or anything else. *(In this one, because it's so abstract, it might just be best to have someone, hands in air or head bowed in prayer, in some kind of worship position)*

One, Two. . .
Two gods is one god too many. I'm jealous. I admit it. So I don't want you making statues of birds or animals or trees and bowing down before them. I want you to worship me. *(Someone bowing down before an idol)*

One, Two, Three. . .
There are three things you should never do with my name. Use it to curse someone. Use it to make promises you don't intend to keep. And use it like it was a joke. I'm special. So is my name. Treat it with respect. *(Perhaps someone cursing/yelling at someone else or maybe making a promise with fingers crossed – anachronistic, I know)*

One, Two, Three, Four. . .
For six days I worked to make the earth. But on the seventh day, I rested. You need to rest as well. So do it on the seventh day, like me. *(Maybe track a character through a working week and then watch him/her rest in the last bit – comic-strip style?)*

One, Two, Three, Four, Five. . .
Alive? You want to stay alive? You want to thrive? Then honour your mother and father. Respect your family. You need them to survive. *(Character helping parents? Hugging parents?)*

One, Two, Three, Four, Five, Six. . .
Sticks and stones really will break your bones. And kicks and punches are only the start of the violence that will break somebody's heart. So no murdering. *(Someone beating up someone else)*

One, Two, Three, Four, Five, Six, Seven. . .
And for heaven's sake, keep your promises. If you marry someone, be faithful to them, body and soul, for the rest of your life. Don't go off with somebody else. *(A picture of a wedding)*

One, Two, Three, Four, Five, Six, Seven, Eight. . .
I hate it when people take other people's stuff. And you should too. It hurts. It makes life hard. So don't steal. *(Someone stealing something, running away: 'Stop, thief!')*

One, Two, Three, Four, Five, Six, Seven, Eight, Nine. . .
There's nothing fine about lying. So don't make up stories about people just to get them into trouble. Tell the truth. *(Someone pointing an accusing finger at someone else – the other person shaking his/her head)*

One, Two, Three, Four, Five, Six, Seven, Eight, Nine and Ten
You could spend and spend and spend and spend! But if you want to live a happy life, be satisfied with what you already have. Don't waste your time wishing you had your neighbour's house, or your neighbour's wife, or your neighbour's things. It will only make you miserable. *(Someone looking longingly at someone else's stuff – comic-trip style again?)*

'One, Two, Three, Four, Five, Six, Seven, Eight, Nine and Ten,' God said.
And now we've reached the end!

? At this point, you could go one of two ways. You could sit everyone back down again and talk to them about the ways in which this story of freedom was a kind of hint at what God would do through Jesus, when he came to set the whole world free. The death of a son (God's not Pharaoh's) that brought about the freedom. The journey through the water as a picture of baptism. The transition from one kind of life (enslaved to sin) to the freedom we have as a part of God's kingdom. That will help them to see the part that this story plays in God's Big Story.

But you might want to go in another direction. As I suggested earlier, this story could very well lead into a discussion of modern slavery. There are, after all, more slaves in the world today than at any other time in history. If you want information about that, you can visit stopthetraffic.org and find all you need. You will also find a story that I have written about a boy named Chaga, who is trapped on a cocoa plantation on the Ivory Coast. Reading this story (there are even cutout masks, drawn by my brother, for the children to make and wear) could be an effective way of bringing the sadness and desperation of slavery home to your group. And also a way of focusing on the hope that we can bring to that situation.

Whatever teaching you choose, finish by singing a quiet song or two, thanking God for setting us free.

SCRIPT

 God's children in slavery (Exodus 1)

Abraham (whom we met last time) had a son named Isaac – remember? *(You might even see if anyone remembers what his name meant)* Isaac had two sons, Jacob and Esau, who didn't get along very well. There was nothing to laugh about there. God changed Jacob's name to Israel, and he had twelve sons. The most famous of them all was Joseph, who went to Egypt and with God's help saved both the Egyptians and his own family from starvation. And there the children of Israel multiplied, until there were loads and loads and loads of them.

The Bible says that one day a man came to rule Egypt, a pharaoh, who did not remember what Joseph had done for his people. He was worried about the children of Israel – worried that there were so many of them. So he turned them into his slaves and set them to work, building his great cities.

That's why we're wearing these chains on our wrists: to remind us that they were slaves and could not escape.

But there are different kinds of slavery, aren't there? Can anyone raise their hand and tell me? *(Hopefully someone tries to raise a hand)* See, you can't do it, can you? The chains mean you have to raise both hands – you can't do what you want to do. You're under somebody or something else's control. *(Discuss different kinds of slavery. These might include sin, bad habits, addictions, and someone might even mention modern forms of slavery.)*

When the children of Israel were enslaved, they cried out to God, and that's how we will start our time together.

 God's help in times of trouble

 Help us, Lord

 Part 1: Exodus (Exodus 5–15)

God heard his people's cry for freedom, and he sent a man named Moses to lead them out of slavery. With God's help, Moses fought with Pharaoh, bringing plague after plague on the people of Egypt. Hail and gnats and frogs and more – ten plagues altogether. And then, after the final plague, when the firstborn children of Egypt died, Pharaoh let the people of Israel go. Or so it seemed. For at the last moment, Pharaoh changed his mind

---

and sent his army to bring them back. The people of Israel were trapped. The Egyptian army was behind them and the Red Sea was in front of them. All hope was lost. And then in one final mighty act of freedom, God told Moses to lift his staff. The waters of the Red Sea parted and the children of Israel walked through. But when Pharaoh's army tried to follow, the waters crashed down around them and they drowned. The children of Israel were free.

So stand up and lift your hands in the air, and on the count of ten – for those ten plagues – I want you to tear off your chains. Are you ready? One, two, three, four, five, six, seven, eight, nine, ten. TEAR OFF YOUR CHAINS!

 God saves us and sets us free

 Part 2: Exodus (Exodus 19)

So God set his people free. But he wanted them to stay free as well, and he wanted to remind them that they were his people, descendents of their father, Abraham, whom he'd called to follow him all those years ago, and the people through whom he intended to bless the world. Remember? That's the promise he'd made to Abraham. All part of the promise he'd made to Adam and Eve. And God keeps his promises.

So just as he sent ten plagues to set them free, he gave them ten rules to keep them free – and to keep them close to him. We call them the Ten Commandments, and we're going to have a look at them now.

 Ten Commandments

 Part 3: Exodus (Exodus 20)

Three months after God's people left Egypt, they came to a mountain called Sinai.

Thunder crashed! Lightning flashed! *(Crash! Flash!)* And with a trumpet blast *(Toot!)*, God came down upon the mountain in a cloud of fire and smoke.

The mountain trembled, like a volcano about to burst.

And God's people trembled too.

Then God called to Moses from the cloud, and Moses climbed the mountain to meet him. 'I want you to talk to my people,' God said. 'My people, whom I rescued from the land of Egypt. The whole world is mine, but they are my special people. A people for all the world to see. A people through whom I will bless the world. And if they are to be my special people, then this is how they must live:

One. . .

There is only one God. That's me. And you mustn't give your hearts to anyone or anything else.

One, Two. . .

Two gods is one god too many. I'm jealous. I admit it. So I don't want you making statues of birds or animals or trees and bowing down before them. I want you to worship me.

One, Two, Three. . .

There are three things you should never do with my name. Use it to curse someone. Use it to make promises you don't intend to keep. And use it like it was a joke. I'm special. So is my name. Treat it with respect.

One, Two, Three, Four. . .

For six days I worked to make the earth. But on the seventh day, I rested. You need to rest as well. So do it on the seventh day, like me.

One, Two, Three, Four, Five. . .

Alive? You want to stay alive? You want to thrive? Then honour your mother and father. Respect your family. You need them to survive.

One, Two, Three, Four, Five, Six. . .

Sticks and stones really will break your bones. And kicks and punches are only the start of the violence that will break somebody's heart. So no murdering.

One, Two, Three, Four, Five, Six, Seven. . .

And for heaven's sake, keep your promises. If you marry someone, be faithful to them, body and soul, for the rest of your life. Don't go off with somebody else.

One, Two, Three, Four, Five, Six, Seven, Eight. . .
I hate it when people take other people's stuff. And you should too. It hurts. It makes life hard. So don't steal.

One, Two, Three, Four, Five, Six, Seven, Eight, Nine. . .
There's nothing fine about lying. So don't make up stories about people just to get them into trouble. Tell the truth.

One, Two, Three, Four, Five, Six, Seven, Eight, Nine and Ten
You could spend and spend and spend and spend! But if you want to live a happy life, be satisfied with what you already have. Don't waste your time wishing you had your neighbour's house, or your neighbour's wife, or your neighbour's things. It will only make you miserable.

'One, Two, Three, Four, Five, Six, Seven, Eight, Nine and Ten,' God said. And now we've reached the end!

Storytelling options:

I have done a lot of retellings of the Exodus story over the years. As an alternative to the telling in this service, you could adapt my retellings in The Lion Storyteller Bible *or the retellings that were used at Spring Harvest several years ago and which can be found in my book* Telling the Bible. *There won't be time for all of them in the space of this service, but the one about the bricks and then the one about the plagues would cover the same territory that I have covered here.*

 Foretelling freedom through Jesus, or present-day slavery

 Thank God for setting us free

CROSSING THE JORDAN

In advance

Prepare dancers or drama team to present the story of the twelve spies. *(Equipment)* Blue ribbon, stones, treats (cakes, fruit, coffee, etc.), large purple balls.

Outline

1st In the desert

♪ Thank God for our freedom and promise of a wonderful home

📖 Part 1: Crossing the Jordan (Numbers 10–11)

🤸 Pet peeves

📖 Part 2: Crossing the Jordan (Numbers 13)

🎭 Spies sent out

♪ Twelve men went to spy

📖 Part 3: Crossing the Jordan (Numbers 14; Joshua 3–4)

❓ Show gratitude to God

🤸 Cross into the promised land

♪ Gratitude to God

🕯 Thank you, God

🤸 Party!

1st This is going to sound all wrong, but you want to start this service by making everyone as uncomfortable as possible and you're going to do it by dividing the space in your building into two parts. There will be the part where you will stand, which will be spacious and littered with all kinds of lovely treats: cakes and sweets and fruit and some nice-smelling coffee or whatever you think smells nice if you're not a coffee fan! And the other area, behind a blue ribbon and a long row of stones (or even bricks) running parallel with the ribbon, is the place where everyone else will spend the bulk of the service. Don't make it unbearable, but based on the number of people who usually attend your services, make it squashed enough that folk will have to sit really close to one another, with absolutely no room to spare. Cram 'em in there! And no, they can't have any cakes. But you (and the band and your helpers) should munch on one from time to time – and really rub it in. Yummm! Why the 'torture'? Because they will be playing the children of Israel, en route in the desert. And you will be speaking to them from the Promised Land! So pluck a few grapes, pop them in your mouth and then say something like this: 'When God set the children of Israel free, he promised to lead them back to the land from which their ancestors, Abraham, Isaac and Jacob, had come. To a land that he said was flowing with milk and honey. But they had to cross a desert first, and that is the journey you will be making today. You're in the desert and I (and the band, etc.) am here in the Promised Land.'

🎵 So let's start our time together where the children of Israel did: thanking God for the freedom he gave them and the promise of a wonderful home. Sing a few songs together that do just that.

📖 When the songs have finished, tell the group that they have two very important contributions to make to the story. They have to complain and they have to die. Very nice!

Tell them that there will be a series of complaints, and that they should start with quiet grumbling and increase the volume with every complaint. Have them practise their complaining. Tell them that they will also have to die, in a Mexican wave fashion, from your left to your right. Tell them to be as dramatic as possible: heads lolling, tongues hanging out, the odd death rattling sound. And then they will have to come to life again, in a Mexican wave fashion, from your right to your left. Practise that as well.

The story is in the Story Box on page 56.

The children of Israel were free. You'd think they would have been happy, grateful, ecstatic even. But it didn't take long for them to start complaining.

When they got hungry, they complained. *(Complaining sounds)*
When they got thirsty, they complained. *(Complain)*
When they got frightened, they complained. *(Complain)*
When Moses went up the mountain to talk with God and didn't come straight back, they complained. *(Complain)*
And on and on and on it went.
'Why have you brought us here?'
'Where are we going?'
'Why didn't we just stay in Egypt?'
They complained. *(Complain)*
And complained. *(Complain)*
And complained. *(Complain)*

Now stop and ask: 'What kind of thing do you complain about? Everybody has what are called pet peeves: things that happen or that people do that frustrate them or make them angry.' Tell one of your pet peeves as an example. Ask everyone to take a minute or two to share one of their pet peeves with the person sitting next to them. Then when they have finished sharing with each other, ask for a few suggestions. You might even want a show of hands after each one. 'Does this get up your nose too?'

Now back to the story: Finally, the children of Israel reached the borders of the Promised Land. But even then, all they could do was complain. *(Big complain)*
   'It will be fine,' Moses tried to assure them. God has promised us this land and he will see to it that we possess it.' And twelve spies were sent into the land to scope it out.

At this point, I think it would be huge fun to put some dancers to work (we haven't given them much to do up to now). They should play the spies, creeping into the Promised Land, all dancer-like, maybe even dressed up in contemporary spy gear: big trench coats and fedoras, Humphrey Bogart style, or in tuxes like James Bond. You could even play James Bond music in the background or the Pink Panther theme! You could have small children on bigger people's shoulders, scary masks over their faces, to play the giants. And maybe some other kids holding big purple balls (for the giant bunches of grapes)! And even if you don't have dancers, you probably have people who can 'move' well enough to pull this off and have a bit of fun. Oh, and if you don't have twelve spies, don't worry. People can use their imagination.

When the drama is finished, just to hammer the point home, why not sing that old song? You know the one:

Twelve men went to spy on Canaan.
Ten were bad and two were good.
What did they see when they got to Canaan?
Ten were bad and two were good.
Some saw giants big and tall.
Some saw grapes in clusters fall.
Some saw God reign over all.
Ten were bad and two were good.

Carry on with the story from the Story Box.

So the spies came back with their report. Ten of the spies were so frightened by the giants that they told the people they would never be able to move into that land. It was just too dangerous. But two of the spies, Joshua and Caleb, said that God would help them, no matter how big the giants were. The children of Israel believed what the ten spies said. And then what did they do? You guessed it! They complained. *(Big complaining)*

'Why have you brought us here?'
'They're going to kill us!'
'Why didn't we stay in Egypt?'

God was really tired of their complaining by now, so he did a little complaining of his own. 'I'm fed up!' he said (or words to that effect). 'I defeated Pharaoh. I gave you your freedom. I fed you in the desert. I provided water for you to drink. I led you in the day and in the night. And all you can do is complain! You're obviously not that keen on going into the land that I have promised you, so here is what will happen. You will wander about in the desert for 40 years. And when the generation that I freed from Egypt has passed on, I will let the rest enter the Promised Land. Except for Joshua and Caleb, that is. They trust me, so they shall enter too.'

And so, for 40 years, the children of Israel wandered in the desert. And when those who had escaped from Egypt were dead *(do Mexican wave dying thing)*, their children, who were still alive *(Mexican wave them alive again in the opposite direction)*, prepared to enter the land. They came to the Jordan River, which was on the border of the Promised Land, and just as they were about to complain that they couldn't get across it, Joshua said, 'Wait just a minute. God has given me a clever plan. Do you remember the stories? The stories of how your parents crossed the Red Sea? How Moses raised his staff and the waters parted and they just walked across? Well, God still has those water-parting powers, and to show you that he is the same God who set your parents free, he is going to part the waters again!'

The priests went first, carrying the Ark of the Covenant, a special box that contained Moses' staff and the Ten Commandments. The people watched eagerly, and as soon as the priests' feet touched the river, the waters parted and they walked across on dry ground.

The people followed, and some of them reached down and picked up stones, and when everyone had reached the other side, they took twelve of those stones – one for each of Israel's sons, one for each of their twelve tribes – and built an altar, so they would never forget to thank God for the amazing things he had done for them.

? Now you want to do some teaching.

'It's easy to complain, isn't it? Life isn't perfect. There are no perfect Christians or perfect churches. People will disappoint us and let us down and hurt us. There's lots to complain about. But sometimes, when we are complaining, we forget all about the good things we have, and the good things people have done for us, and the good things God has done for us as well. And we find ourselves wandering about in a desert of bitterness and unhappiness – hopefully not for 40 years, but sometimes for a long time.

'There is a way to deal with that, and that is the way the children of Israel discovered. The way God showed them. And that way is the way of gratitude. It's to remember all those good things that have happened and to say thank you for them.'

⚡ 'So that's what we're going to do now. We're going to leave the desert of complaining and cross over to the Promised Land of thankfulness. And this is how we are going to do it. The band is going to play something quiet, and for a little while all I want you to do is to think and to remember something that God has done for you, something you are thankful for. And when you have thought of that, pick up a stone and cross the river.' (As soon as someone touches the ribbon, it should fall – like the river parted – so they are able to cross.) 'When you have entered the Promised Land, set the stone on the floor and if you like (only one at a time, please) you can tell the rest of us what you are thankful for. We will carry on as long as there are stones and thanks and people want to speak, but if you don't want to speak, don't worry. Just set your stone down and listen to the others. God shows his love for us through other people as well. Maybe there is someone in this room whom he has used to do that for you. You can tell them that if you like, and take their hand and cross the river with them. Pick up a stone together.'

Now let the music play and just wait. When I did this service, it took a little while for the first person to speak. Be patient. This is a big 'ask' and it might take time. But it turned out to be a very moving experience for our folk, and I think there's a good chance it will for yours as well.

When everyone has 'crossed over' have the band lead them in a quiet song of gratitude to God.

End this section with a prayer of gratitude.

Now give a big grin and say, 'Well, looks as if we're in the Promised Land at last! A land flowing with milk and honey – that's what God called it. We don't have a lot of milk here and not much honey either' (unless of course you do) 'but there are loads of cakes and sweets and fruit and drinks. So why don't we celebrate by eating and drinking them up!'

Then let 'em at it! They'll have been drooling during the whole service anyway. So party! Have the band kick into something big and noisy as well, so some can sing and some can eat and everyone can enjoy the noise and the excitement (except for those, of course, who will inevitably complain to each other about it afterwards!).

SCRIPT

 In the desert

When God set the children of Israel free, he promised to lead them back to the land from which their ancestors, Abraham, Isaac and Jacob, had come. To a land that he said was flowing with milk and honey. But they had to cross a desert first, and that is the journey you will be making today. You're in the desert and I (and the band, etc.) am here in the Promised Land.

 Thank God for our freedom and promise of a wonderful home

 Part 1: Crossing the Jordan (Numbers 10–11)

Practise complaining and Mexican waves.
The children of Israel were free. You'd think they would have been happy, grateful, ecstatic even. But it didn't take long for them to start complaining.
When they got hungry, they complained. *(Complaining sounds)*
When they got thirsty, they complained. *(Complain)*
When they got frightened, they complained. *(Complain)*
When Moses went up the mountain to talk with God and didn't come straight back, they complained. *(Complain)*
And on and on and on it went.
'Why have you brought us here?'
'Where are we going?'
'Why didn't we just stay in Egypt?'
They complained. *(Complain)*
And complained. *(Complain)*
And complained. *(Complain)*

 Pet peeves

What kind of thing do you complain about? Everybody has what are called pet peeves: things that happen or that people do that frustrate them or make them angry.

Tell one of your pet peeves as an example.

Take a minute or two to share one of your pet peeves with the person sitting next to you.

Ask for a few suggestions.

Does this get up your nose too?

 Part 2: Crossing the Jordan (Numbers 13)

Finally, the children of Israel reached the borders of the Promised Land. But even then, all they could do was complain. *(Big complain)*

'It will be fine,' Moses tried to assure them. 'God has promised us this land and he will see to it that we possess it.' And twelve spies were sent into the land to scope it out.

 Spies sent out

 'Twelve men went to spy'

 Part 3: Crossing the Jordan (Numbers 14; Joshua 3–4)

So the spies came back with their report. Ten of the spies were so frightened by the giants that they told the people they would never be able to move into that land. It was just too dangerous. But two of the spies, Joshua and Caleb, said that God would help them, no matter how big the giants were. The children of Israel believed what the ten spies said. And then what did they do? You guessed it! They complained. *(Big complaining)*

'Why have you brought us here?'
'They're going to kill us!'
'Why didn't we stay in Egypt?'

God was really tired of their complaining by now, so he did a little complaining of his own. 'I'm fed up!' he said (or words to that effect). 'I defeated Pharaoh. I gave you your freedom. I fed you in the desert. I provided water for you to drink. I led you in the day and in the night.

And all you can do is complain! You're obviously not that keen on going into the land that I have promised you, so here is what will happen. You will wander about in the desert for 40 years. And when the generation that I freed from Egypt has passed on, I will let the rest enter the Promised Land. Except for Joshua and Caleb, that is. They trust me, so they shall enter too.

And so, for 40 years, the children of Israel wandered in the desert. And when those who had escaped from Egypt were dead *(do Mexican wave dying thing)*, their children, who were still alive *(Mexican wave them alive again in the opposite direction)*, prepared to enter the land. They came to the Jordan River, which was on the border of the Promised Land, and just as they were about to complain that they couldn't get across it, Joshua said, 'Wait just a minute. God has given me a clever plan. Do you remember the stories? The stories of how your parents crossed the Red Sea? How Moses raised his staff and the waters parted and they just walked across? Well, God still has those water-parting powers, and to show you that he is the same God who set your parents free, he is going to part the waters again!'

The priests went first, carrying the Ark of the Covenant, a special box that contained Moses' staff and the Ten Commandments. The people watched eagerly, and as soon as the priests' feet touched the river, the waters parted and they walked across on dry ground.

The people followed, and some of them reached down and picked up stones, and when everyone had reached the other side, they took twelve of those stones – one for each of Israel's sons, one for each of their twelve tribes – and built an altar, so they would never forget to thank God for the amazing things he had done for them.

 Show gratitude to God

It's easy to complain, isn't it? Life isn't perfect. There are no perfect Christians or perfect churches. People will disappoint us and let us down and hurt us. There's lots to complain about. But sometimes, when we are complaining, we forget all about the good things we have, and the good things people have done for us, and the good things God has done for us as well. And we find ourselves wandering about in a desert of bitterness and unhappiness – hopefully not for 40 years, but sometimes for a long time.

There is a way to deal with that, and that is the way that the children of Israel discovered. The way God showed them. And that way is the way of gratitude. It's to remember all those good things that have happened and to say thank you for them.

 Cross into the Promised Land

So that's what we're going to do now. We're going to leave the desert of complaining and cross over to the Promised Land of thankfulness. And this is how we are going to do it. The band is going to play something quiet, and for a little while all I want you to do is to think and to remember something that God has done for you, something you are thankful for. And when you have thought of that, pick up a stone and cross the river. When you have entered the Promised Land, set the stone on the floor and if you like (only one at a time, please) you can tell the rest of us what you are thankful for. We will carry on as long as there are stones and thanks and people want to speak, but if you don't want to speak, don't worry. Just set your stone down and listen to the others. God shows his love for us through other people as well. Maybe there is someone in this room whom he has used to do that for you. You can tell them that, if you like, and take their hand and cross the river with them. Pick up a stone together.

 Gratitude to God

 Thank you, God

 Party!

NEHEMIAH

In advance

Hang paper gates around the room, label them and put appropriate craft materials by each one.

🗄 Large strips of paper; blu-tack; craft materials.

Outline

1st Meet Nehemiah

📖 Part 1: Nehemiah (Nehemiah 1)

🔥 Nehemiah's prayer (Nehemiah 1:5–11)

🎵 God is faithful, just and forgiving

📖 Part 2: Nehemiah (Nehemiah 2)

🤸 Rebuild the gates

❓ Inviting people in

🔥 The ways into church

🎵 Recommitment to God

1st Here's the thing. You have to keep your group on their toes. You have to do something unexpected – like that 'surprise and delight' thing that car manufacturers are always going on about. You know: the cupholder that pops out of some secret place on the dashboard and unfolds itself like some amazing bit of automotive origami.

This is especially true for those Bible stories that your group knows well. There's nothing worse than the 'been there, done that' atmosphere that seeps into the room at the start of a familiar Bible story. And that's because the Bible simply isn't a 'been there, done that' kind of book. It's a journey, an amazing adventure. And it deserves to be told like that.

As it happens, you probably won't get those 'been there, done that' looks when this story begins, because it's not all that familiar. But you still need to make sure that your group is set up to expect an adventure, even as they walk into the room.

The story is all about rebuilding the gates of Jerusalem, so you're going to need some gates. Now maybe you have some gates, some real gates. That's cool, but you're going to need nine of them, and that's a lot. So why not save yourself some time and trouble and expense and make some paper gates? Not so good for keeping Sanballat and Co. out of the city, granted, but perfectly adequate for telling the story.

Get some strips of paper, say three feet wide by seven or eight feet long, and hang them on the walls around the room. Blu-tack should work just fine. But ask first.

Label each gate in big chunky letters (preferably before you stick the paper to the walls).

You'll need a Fish gate, a Sheep gate, an Old gate, a Muster gate, a Valley gate, a Dung gate (yeah, really!), a Fountain gate, a Water gate, an East gate and a Horse gate.

Start with the Fish gate, front and centre, and then hang the gates as close as you can in the positions they stood round the walls of Jerusalem. Use the illustration below, if that helps, or check out a Bible commentary.

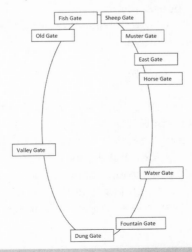

The idea is to give some sense of the setting of the story, because if you know where you are in a story, it helps you to understand what the story is all about. Think Narnia without the lamppost and the wintry wood, or *Lord of the Rings* without those little hobbit houses. The place makes a difference, doesn't it?

And that's why there's no point in you doing all the work, where the setting is concerned. You 'get' the story partly because of all the work you put into envisioning it and preparing for it. So it makes sense that your group will 'get' it better if they do some work as well. So put a table at the foot of each gate, and fill the table with whatever craft material you can beg or borrow (no, stealing is not an option here – you're in church, for heaven's sake!). Chunky markers, cloth, netting, coloured paper – that's what you're looking for. And lots of glue sticks.

Now it's time to bring your group into the room. And the first thing you do, once they get settled, is ignore the tables and the paper gates altogether. That's right, you want them to sit there just wondering what this is all about. Because the wondering will lead to questions.

And questions are exactly what you want!

'What's going on here?'

'What's the paper for?'

'Where are we going today?'

'When does the children's minister's contract expire?'

That sort of thing.

Is everyone now in the room? Is everyone seated? Now is the time to start the story!

Divide everyone into two groups. Tell one group that they are to play Nehemiah, waving and saying 'hello' with you (in a deep and manly voice) whenever you say 'man' or 'Nehemiah'. The other group plays 'his people' and does the same (but not necessarily in a manly voice – there were ladies too!) when you say 'his people' or 'Jews'. Have everyone frown and say 'Aww!' with you when you say 'without a prayer'.

See the Story Box on page 65.

 Now is the time to pray. And the prayer you will pray is Nehemiah's prayer. You might like to ask someone else to read it. The change of voice will be helpful. You might prefer a summary of the prayer or a reading from a modern translation. But whatever you do, make sure it's read well. No rushing through or droning on. It's key that your group really hears the prayer and understands what it's about; that they hear it and pray along with it as if it's their prayer too. In fact, you might like to ask them to close their eyes and bow their heads as it's read. Or you might like to ask them to repeat a simple line or two from the prayer, along with the person who is reading it, so it becomes their prayer as well.

Once the prayer is finished, use what the prayer has to say about God (he is faithful, he is just, he is forgiving) to sing a few songs to him.

When you have finished singing, it's time to get back to the story:
Tell your groups that the participation will be much the same as before (one side 'hello-ing' with Nehemiah, the other side 'hello-ing' with the Jews). But instead of frowning and saying 'Aww!' because they 'haven't got a prayer' they need to smile and cheer because they now 'have a prayer' at last. Oh, and they all need to grimace and make a poisoned/dying/ackking sound with you when the 'cup' is mentioned! Continue with the story on pages 66–67.

So now is the time to rebuild the city. Tell everyone to split up into nine groups and, using the craft materials, decorate the big sheets of paper (having taken them off the wall) to make them look like the gates of Jerusalem. Tell them to use the name of each gate as a clue to how their gate should be decorated. For example, they could cut out lots of paper fish and stick them to the Fish gate; some netting as well, perhaps. Puffy cotton-wool sheep for the Sheep gate. You get the idea – though I'll leave it to you how best to provide direction for the Dung gate!

Let people split up however they like. You may have some groups with just children, some with just teens or adults, and some with a mix. Tell them it's important that everyone gets the chance to add something to their gate, however small. And give them plenty of time to do a really nice job – 20 minutes, or even more if everyone is really getting into it. Your job, during this process, is to wander around the room encouraging and offering advice (serious and less so). If you have some folk who aren't keen on the craft thing at all, and are just sitting and doing nothing, there is a list of questions about the story that they might like to answer either in a small group or individually (see pages 67–68 for the questions). But don't offer this as an alternative at first. You want as many as possible to engage in the activity.

Once the gates are finished, hang them back on the walls in their original places, and then have the people in the room fill in the spaces between the gates. If you have chairs, they can move the chairs from the middle of the room to the edges, and then sit down on them. If you have pews, they can stand or sit between the gates. But they need to become the wall – that's the key thing – even if you have to double up and make the wall two or three people deep (kids in front, please, if that's the case).

? Now you want to spend a little time looking at the gates, giving everyone the chance to admire everyone else's work. You might like to go gate by gate around the room and give the gate-makers the opportunity to make a few short comments about why they did what they did.

When that is finished, you want to ask a simple question: 'Why did Nehemiah and his people need to rebuild the walls and gates? The answer is quite simple, isn't it? They needed to keep their enemies out.'

Then follow up with this question: 'We're a church. We don't want to keep people out. We want them to come in. What if these gates, these gates we have just built, were not the gates of Jerusalem – gates to keep people out – but gates into our church; gates to bring people in? What would each of these gates stand for?'

Then go round the gates again. Maybe the Fish gate would be 'evangelism' – fishers of men! Maybe the Dung gate would stand for doing hard things in our community, the getting-our-hands-dirty things that help people day by day. Give an opportunity for people to think out loud about each gate.

◐ When that is done, take some time to pray, either all together or in your little gate-making groups, about the ways into your church.

♫ When the walls were finished, Nehemiah and his people worshipped God and recommitted themselves to him. Remind everyone of that and then have another time of worship in singing.

This would also be an appropriate time to collect the offering.

And that's it, really. Your story finishes when Nehemiah's does. Leave the gates where they are and send everyone out of the room (with the encouragement, perhaps, to bring someone new through those gates the following week).

SCRIPT

 Meet Nehemiah

 Part 1: Nehemiah (Nehemiah 1)

Divide everyone into two groups. Tell one group that they are to play Nehemiah, waving and saying 'hello' with you (in a deep and manly voice) whenever you say 'man' or 'Nehemiah'. The other group plays 'his people' and does the same (but not necessarily in a manly voice – there were ladies too) when you say 'his people' or 'Jews'. Have everyone frown and say 'Aww!' with you when you say 'without a prayer'.

Once there was a man, (*Nehemiahs wave & hello*)
A man with a people, (*Nehemiahs wave & hello / People wave & hello*)
A people without a prayer. (*People wave & hello / All aww*)

The man was Nehemiah. (*N hello*)
His people were the Jews (*P hello*)
And they didn't have a prayer, (*aww*)
Because when they returned from exile
To their special city, Jerusalem,
They found it in ruins.
The walls were knocked down,
The gates were shattered
And their enemies surrounded them.

Once there was a man, (*N hello*)
A man with a people, (*N hello / P hello*)
A people without a prayer. (*P hello / aww*)
So what did Nehemiah do? (*N hello*)
Hundreds of miles away, in the court of King Artaxerxes?
He gave them a prayer – that's what.
And this is what he prayed.

 Nehemiah's prayer (Nehemiah 1:5–11)

 God is faithful, just and forgiving

Part 2: Nehemiah (Nehemiah 2)

Tell your groups that the participation will be much the same as before (one side 'hello-ing' with Nehemiah, the other side 'hello-ing' with the Jews). But instead of frowning and saying 'Aww!' because they 'haven't got a prayer' they need to smile and cheer because they now 'have a prayer' at last. Oh, and they all need to grimace and make a poisoned/dying/ackking sound with you when the 'cup' is mentioned!

Once there was a man, (*N hello*)
A man with a people, (*N hello / P hello*)
A man with a prayer (*N hello / cheer*)
And a man with a cup, as well. (*N hello / acck*)

The man was Nehemiah, (*N hello*)
His people were the Jews, (*P hello*)
His prayer gave him strength. (*Cheer*)
And his cup, (*Acck*)
His cup was the cup of a king, (*Acck*)
For Nehemiah was the cupbearer of Artaxerxes, King of Persia. (*N hello*)

This was no ordinary job.
When the king sat down to eat
Nehemiah would bring him his cup. (*N hello*)
He would taste it first,
Taste whatever was in it,
So that if the cup was poisoned
Nehemiah would die (*N hello*)
And not the king.
And what is more
Nehemiah would have to do this with a smile on his face, (*N hello*)
So that it looked as if nothing on earth might be wrong.

Well, when Nehemiah had prayed his prayer (*N hello / cheer*)
He went in with a cup to the king,
But because of the sorry state of his people (*P hello*)
He did not have a smile on his face.

The king was worried.
With no smile on his cupbearer's face,
What, he wondered, was waiting for him in the cup?
And that is why he asked, 'What's wrong, Nehemiah?' (*N hello*)
And that is when Nehemiah told the king (*N hello*)
About his people's troubles. (*P hello*)
Their walls are knocked down,
Their gates are shattered,
Their enemies surround them.

And that is when Nehemiah asked for the king's help: (*N hello*)
– a leave of absence to go to Jerusalem
– safe passage through the lands in between
– and a lorry load of timber to fix the city gates.
It was a big request,
But Nehemiah had prayed. (*N hello / cheer*)
God was faithful
And so the king said 'yes'!

So now there was a man, (*N hello*)
A man with a people, (*N hello / P hello*)
A people with a prayer, (*P hello / cheer*)
Who put down his cup, (*Acck*)
Picked up his passport
And a load of timber,
And set off to rebuild the city of Jerusalem.

 Rebuild the gates

Activity alternative questions:
Read Nehemiah chapter 1 and chapter 2:1–10

1. *Describe the message that Nehemiah receives from Hanani.*
2. *What is Nehemiah's response to the message?*
3. *What does Nehemiah's prayer say about God? What does it say about his people? What does Nehemiah ask for?*

4. How many times does the text mention that Nehemiah prays in chapters 1 and 2?
5. What is Nehemiah's job? What does that job entail?
6. Why is Nehemiah afraid when the king notices that he is sad? How does he deal with that fear? Do you think that Nehemiah is a brave man? Name two or three other biblical characters who had to overcome their fear to do what God wanted them to do.
7. What does Nehemiah ask of the king?
8. Talk about a time when God asked you to do something that you were afraid to do. How did you deal with the fear?
9. Is there any challenge that you or your church are facing right now that requires a Nehemiah kind of prayer?

 Inviting people in

Give the gate-makers the opportunity to make a few short comments about why they did what they did.

Why did Nehemiah and his people need to rebuild the walls and gates? The answer is quite simple, isn't it? They needed to keep their enemies out.

We're a church. We don't want to keep people out. We want them to come in. What if these gates, these gates we have just built, were not the gates of Jerusalem – gates to keep people out – but gates into our church; gates to bring people in? What would each of these gates stand for?

Go round the gates again. Maybe the Fish gate would be 'evangelism' – fishers of men! Maybe the Dung gate would stand for doing hard things in our community, the getting-our-hands-dirty things that help people day by day. Give people an opportunity to think out loud about each gate.

 The ways into church

 Recommitment to God

When the walls were finished, Nehemiah and his people worshipped God and recommitted themselves to him.

CHRISTMAS

In advance

Announce the event and ask for people to come dressed as the characters. Set the stage. Arrange for four helpers to be dressed as Mary, Joseph, a shepherd and a donkey (or any animal other than a sheep), and to lead their group.

Outline

1st Who are you?

Carols

Commit the time to God

Part 1: Christmas (Luke 1:26–38; Matthew 1:18–24)

? The courage to do something hard

Following God

Requesting courage to do as God asks

Part 2: Christmas (Luke 2:1–7)

'Away in a manger'

Part 3: Christmas (Luke 2:8–20)

Carols

1st   It's Christmas time and everybody's busy, yeah? And nobody has time to bring the kids to rehearse for the annual Christmas pageant, yeah? So you do your best and muddle through, and in many ways it doesn't actually matter that no one knows their lines or where to stand, because the 'Aww!' factor is there anyway, in the three-year-olds dressed up as little lambs and Mary clutching her baby doll (until Joseph snatches him away and drops him, that is!). But you're still frazzled, yeah? And you still maintain that this is the last year you're doing it – until next year arrives, of course, 'cause if you don't do it, everyone will be SOOO disappointed!

Well here, I hope, is the answer to your prayers: a rehearsal-less Christmas pageant! You can do it as an all-age service. You can do it as a carol service. But however you do it, the whole point of it is that there is no rehearsal. It's a risk, I'll grant you that. It depends largely on the goodwill and graciousness of a big part of your church. Without that, it is most certainly doomed to failure. But look on the bright side. If it works, you'll have pulled off a lovely Christmas service without any of the aggro beforehand. And if it doesn't, they'll never ask you to do it again. Win win!

Before we get started, a wise man warning! There was a woman in the church where I was raised who was particularly fussy about the Wise Man Issue. You know: they weren't at the stable with the shepherds. They visited the baby in a house, sometime later, when he was older. Which is all true, and fair enough. But she had extremely strong feelings about all of this, to the extent that if a nativity set was put up anywhere in the church and it included the wise men, by the following week they would have disappeared! You'd find them at the back of the building, or sitting on a radiator halfway up the aisle. 'They're on their way!' she'd explain. 'But they're not there yet.' Perhaps this lady goes to your church too (I suspect that every church has one). If so, she will be delighted with this service, because it is not only rehearsal-less, it is magi-free. Not because I have any particular theological compunctions, but because it makes things even more complicated and doesn't fit my thematic structure. So there!

Finally, there is one last potential difficulty with this service. In order for it to work, everybody has to dress up. Well, nearly everybody. Because it's a fancy dress Christmas pageant. I know what you're thinking: they'll never do it! And that's what I thought the first time I did it. So I was prepared to use however many people came willing to play along. And you probably need to be prepared for that as well. But, boy, did my church shock me. The level of participation was fantastic. The people streamed into the church in their bathrobes and towels and woolly lamb's ears – it was an amazing sight. And there was a real buzz even before the service began. There was one elderly gentleman in particular, whose son had worked in the Middle East. So Stan, who was well past 80, appeared that morning dressed in full Arab regalia – an inspiration to us all. Frankly, I don't think we give our people enough credit sometimes. We're the ones who worry about how they will react, and that worry rubs off on them. Plus, if you have been doing these stories in order, and not just picking and choosing (a lot of thought went into the sequence, in case you hadn't noticed), then they will have already done plenty of uncomfortable things and hopefully enjoyed them. So this won't be too much of a stretch.

Two or three weeks before this service, you need to announce that you want everyone to come to this year's carol service/all-age Christmas service dressed up as a character from the Christmas story. Then tell them the specific characters you need. This will spare you from having to find a place in your story for Rudolph the Red-Nosed Reindeer, as we had to do once. Hey, we put him in the stable with the donkeys and cows. It worked for me – and his little red nose shone with joy! You want Marys, Josephs, angels (Gabriel will be the star of our show), shepherds and an assortment of animals: sheep and donkeys definitely; other breeds optional. Tell everyone that they are free to make their costumes as simple or elaborate as they like, and that humour is most definitely welcome. A big burly guy with a headband and a couple of woolly socks for ears will make a magnificent sheep and add to the joy (and ridiculousness) of the occasion. Be as playful with this invitation as you can be, and repeat it in the succeeding weeks in the run-up to the event. If you are worried that you will not have sufficient participation, allocate characters to a few trustworthy volunteers so that you know you will have at least one of each of the characters you need. Your helpers will need to be allocated parts too.

Should you set the stage? Yes, if you want to, of course. But I wouldn't make it too cluttered. A simple house/stable shape perhaps. A portable manger, a few hay bales maybe. Nothing fancy. The fun will be in what you do with the story and with your (hopefully) all-encompassing cast of characters.

On the day, have some bright Christmas music playing as everyone enters – live, canned, whatever you've got. But you want to give the sense that this is going to be big and bold and fun. Let everyone mingle and admire (or laugh at) each other's costumes.

Without introduction, burst into some bright, celebratory Christmas carols.

After the singing, tell everyone how incredible they look, thank them for 'having a go' and then give God thanks for Christmas and ask for his help in telling his amazing Christmas story (you're going to need it!).

Now it's time to sort your characters. Ask all your Marys to sit in the front right (your right) quadrant of the room. All the Josephs sit in the front left. All the shepherds and sheep sit in the back right. All the other animals sit in the back left. And all the angels go to the front, sitting or standing behind you. Ideally you will leave enough room at the front for everyone to gather there at the end. If your venue isn't big enough for that, you will need to modify the directions at the end of the story to fit your space.

It's time for everyone to learn their lines and actions. Fortunately, they are all very simple. You could have a slip of paper for each group to read, but it will be easier to have a helper with each group (dressed to fit in with that group, of course), to explain what they have to do.

You work with the angels. They will all be Gabriel, for the sake of simplicity, and their line is 'Surprise!' They shout it to Mary, whisper it to Joseph and really shout it to the shepherds. Simple. They should stand behind you – raised just a bit would be best.

The Marys have the hardest part. They have one line, 'But I don't even have a husband yet!', and they need to nod when the narrator says, 'If that's what God wants, then I'll do it.'

The Josephs have the easiest part, I think. They have to pretend they are asleep (head on folded hands, standing or lying down if there is room). And then they have to shake themselves awake and look surprised.

The shepherds only have to shake with fear (a bit of screaming would be all right too) and the sheep who are with them should 'baaa' in a frightened way.

The other animals simply need to make animal sounds (appropriate to their species) on cue in the stable scene.

Now start telling the story from the Story Box on page 74.

Then ask, 'Has God ever asked you to do something hard? Something difficult? Something you didn't really want to do?' Look for answers from the group. If none are forthcoming, suggest a few: forgive someone who really hurt you. Help somebody you didn't like. Give up something for someone else. That's what both Joseph and Mary did, and we're grateful for that.

Sing a song or two about following God and doing what he asks us to do.

Then lead everyone in a prayer, asking for the courage and strength to do even the hard things God asks.

Continue with the story from page 76.

Sing 'Away in a manger', or something similar that is simple and well known, because you probably won't have arranged for the people up front to see the words (unless you've really thought about it beforehand).

Tell the final part of the story from page 77.

And now you want to sing again. Big, happy carols. Just leave everyone at the front, as long as they can turn around and see the words on the screen. No one is watching anyone now, they are all a part of the story – all a part of the celebration. Which makes perfect sense since God comes to be a part of us. And if in the midst of the celebration you want to release some balloons or throw some confetti, go for it. It's a party now! Just encourage everyone to sing and enjoy.

SCRIPT

 1st *Who are you?*

 Carols

 Commit the time to God

 Part 1: Christmas (Luke 1:26–38; Matthew 1:18–24)

Marys sit at the front right, Josephs sit at the front left, shepherds and sheep sit at the back right, all the other animals sit at the back left and all the angels sit or stand behind you.

The angels' line is 'Surprise!'. They shout it to Mary, whisper it to Joseph and really shout it to the shepherds.

    The Marys have the line 'But I don't even have a husband yet!' and they need to nod when the narrator says, 'If that's what God wants, then I'll do it.'

    The Josephs have to pretend they are asleep and then they have to shake themselves awake and look surprised.

    The shepherds have to shake with fear and the sheep 'baaa' in a frightened way.

    The other animals make animal sounds (appropriate to their species) on cue in the stable scene.

Once there was a girl named Mary, who lived in a town called Nazareth. (*Marys come up to the front*)

    One day the angel Gabriel appeared to her and shouted (*Point to your angels and they shout* 'Surprise!')

And Mary didn't know what to think.
She'd never seen an angel before.
But she was staring at one now!

Gabriel said it again (*Angels:* 'Surprise!') because Gabriel loved surprises.
And this was one of the best.
A warm, pink, cuddly surprise.

'You're going to have a baby!' he announced.
And Mary was, indeed, surprised.
So surprised that she said so. (*Point to Marys and have helper lead:* 'But I don't even have a husband yet!')

'That's the best part,' grinned Gabriel. He couldn't wait to tell her.
'God's own Spirit will wrap himself around you – like the paper on a present, like a blanket on a stormy night – and your baby will be God's baby!'

And now Mary was more surprised than ever. And honoured and humbled too.
'If that's what God wants, then I'll do it,' she said. (*Marys nod*)
And as quickly as he'd come, Gabriel disappeared. (*Angels:* 'Surprise!')

Send the Marys back to their seats with a big clap. Once they are seated, carry on with the story.

Mary was engaged to a man named Joseph. A good man.
Come on, Josephs – get up here!

The Josephs all come forward and stand where the Marys stood, either lying down or with their heads tilted and resting on their folded hands, and their eyes shut as if they are asleep. A bit of snoring is permissable, but it needs to be quiet so that everyone can hear the story.
Joseph was asleep one night, when Gabriel came to him in a dream and whispered (*Angels:* 'Surprise!')

But it was not a nice dream.
No sugar plums. No fairies.
Just empty stockings and lumps of coal.
For Joseph was engaged to Mary.
And Mary was going to have a baby.
And the baby wasn't his.

So once again Gabriel whispered (*Angels:* 'Surprise!')
Because Gabriel loved surprises.
'What Mary has told you is true,' he said.
'She is going to be the mother of God's own special Son.
So believe her, because she loves you.

Marry her, like you promised.
And when the baby is born, call him Jesus, for he is God's best and biggest surprise – come to save the world from all that is wrong.'

And then, before Joseph could shake himself awake (*Josephs wake themselves up with a shake*), the angel disappeared. (*Angels:* 'Surprise!')

Send the Josephs back to their seats with a clap.

 The courage to do something hard

Has God ever asked you to do something hard? Something difficult? Something you didn't really want to do?
   Look for answers from the group. If none are forthcoming, suggest a few: forgive someone who really hurt you. Help somebody you didn't like. Give up something for someone else. That's what both Joseph and Mary did, and we're grateful for that.

 Following God

So let's sing a song about following God and doing what he asks us to do.

 Requesting courage to do as God asks

 Part 2: Christmas (Luke 2:1–7)

So Mary and Joseph were married. But she didn't have her baby in Nazareth. No. Before the baby was born, the emperor, Augustus, said that everyone had to return to their hometown, so that the whole population could be counted. So Joseph took Mary to the town where his ancestors had come from: the town of Bethlehem, miles and miles away. There were so many people there that Joseph and Mary couldn't find a place to stay. But a kindly innkeeper let them stop in the stable behind his inn.
   So come on, Marys. (*Marys come up to the front*)
   Come on, Josephs. (*Josephs come up to the front*)
   And come on, stable animals too. (*Animals come up to the front*)

Let's pair up, a Mary with a Joseph. (*This will depend on the numbers you have and each Joseph may end up with several Marys or vice versa!*)

Now, Marys, cradle a pretend baby in your arms. And let's hear it from the animals. (*Lots of mooing, clucking, hee-hawing, etc.*)

And there it was that Mary gave birth to God's Son, Jesus. And the King of all the world was born, not in a palace, but in a stable. Come to be one of us, just like us, so he could bring us back to God.

 'Away in a manger'

 Part 3: Christmas (Luke 2:8–20)

But Gabriel wasn't finished with his work. Not by a long shot.

He appeared to a bunch of shepherds, watching their sheep on a hill outside Bethlehem.

And what did he say? You know what he said. (*Angels:* 'Surprise!')

And the shiny bright white of his angel face burst the starry blue wrapping of night.

The shepherds were more than surprised. They shivered and shook. (*Shepherds shake, sheep baa*) They were shocked!

Gabriel loved surprises. And because he didn't want to ruin this one, he said very calmly, 'Don't be afraid. I have good news for you. A baby born tonight in Bethlehem is the baby you and all your people have been waiting for. He is the special King God promised to send you.'

And then Gabriel grinned an angel grin. A grin so wide his teeth shone just like stars.

'And here's the best bit,' he grinned. 'You won't find him in a throne room. No. He's lying in an ordinary manger.' (*Angels:* 'Surprise!')

Then angels, like fireworks, shot out of the sky. Silver foil, gold ribbons of light. And Gabriel led them in a song.

'God is amazing! Higher than kings! And peace is the gift he brings!'

And then, as suddenly as they had appeared, Gabriel and the angels were gone. (*Angels:* 'Surprise!')

So the shepherds went off – to find a king in a stable.

> Come on, shepherds. *(Shepherds should walk down the aisle with their sheep and join you at the front)*
>
> And they worshipped the newborn King.

 Carols

THE WRECKED ROOF

In advance

Create a 'house' out of a large cardboard box with a hole cut in the top which is covered by a flimsy 'roof'.

Clay, play-doh; paper; pencils, crayons; computers; digital cameras; printer.

Outline

1st Surprise and friends

This is my friend

Part 1: The wrecked roof (Mark 2:1)

Wanting to be in the presence of Jesus

Thank Jesus for his presence

Part 2: The wrecked roof (Mark 2:2–12)

? Jesus wants to be our friend

Our friends' needs

Jesus, please help our friends

Thank Jesus for being our friend

1st Let's start with a surprise, shall we?

You will need to build a house – one of those flat-roofed New Testament houses, with some painted steps leading up one side and a door and a couple of windows at the front.

Build it out of a big box. And build it big enough that you (or at the very least someone smaller and more nimble) can crouch down and hide inside. Cut a hole in the top of the box, big enough for you (or that smaller, nimbler person) to burst out of. And then cover the hole with a false and flimsy paper roof.

Once everyone has come in and quietened down (you might want to plant a few shushers), burst out of the box and shout 'Surprise!'.

Hopefully you will get some kind of reaction, and when that has died down, ask how your group would feel if somebody had burst through their roof – their roof at home maybe, or the church roof – because there's going to be some roof-wrecking in the story today.

Tell them that there are going to be friends as well. And then introduce them to one of your friends.

If your church is set up for wi-fi and you have a projector hooked up to a computer, you can call up Facebook on the internet and show it to everyone in the room. If you're not a member of Facebook, you need to join in the week before and get yourself some friends, because that's what I want you to show them: a picture of one of your Facebook friends and maybe even a little information from their profile page – name, age (could be tricky), family, likes and dislikes. But just a few.

Then say something like, 'I have friends, and so do you. I've introduced you to my friend. Now I want to meet yours!'

Send everyone off to different stations around the room. One should have clay or play-doh, where they can mould or sculpt something that looks like their friend. One should have paper and pencils or crayons, where they can draw or write something about their friend. Another can be equipped with a couple more computers (lots of supervision at this one!) and a printer, because if they can access the net, they can call up and print off pictures of their Facebook friends. You could also have a station with digital cameras and a photo printer, in case their friend is in the room with them.

Encourage them to add details to their picture, poem, sculpture, etc., like you did: age, family, likes and dislikes. And when they have finished, ask them to take their friends back to their seats with them. Have some quiet music playing in the background during this activity, as you have done on other occasions.

After a while, stop the music and ask a few people to hold up their work and say a thing or two about their friends. Tell them that friends are really important and that good friends would do just about anything for each other, as they will see in the story now.

Tell the first part of the story in the Story Box on pages 83–84.

When the first part of the story is finished, ask your group if they heard anything in the story about a friend, and say, 'That's right – Daniel played with his friends. And Daniel's father was worried about his sick friend.'

Ask them if there were other sick people in the story, and say, 'That's right – they were going to Aaron the Pharisee's house, because Jesus was there.'

Then ask, 'Why don't we ask Jesus to come and be here with us as well!' Sing a few songs about inviting Jesus, and seeing Jesus, and knowing that he's near.

After the singing, lead everyone in a prayer thanking Jesus for being there with you.

Now continue the story from page 85.

Then say just a few things about the story.

Tell them that many years before Jesus was born, a prophet called Isaiah said Jesus' wounds, the hurt he suffered on the cross, would take away the pain of all the bad things that happen to us and the bad things we do – our sickness and our sin. And that's just what Jesus did for the man who was lowered through the roof: he fixed all that was wrong with him.

Jesus himself said that there's no greater thing that someone can do than give his life for his friend. Jesus did that for us, on the cross. He wants to be our friend. And he wants to take care of our friends as well.

Now explain to everyone: 'As the music is playing, we're going to bring our friends up to this house – this house with no roof, just like the one Daniel's dad made. And as we bring them up, you might want to pray for them. Perhaps your friend is having trouble, or is sick, or just needs to know that Jesus wants to be his or her friend too. So pray whatever you like for your friend, and then lower your friend into the house, like Daniel's dad lowered his friend (we'll be here to help you!) and set him before Jesus.'

Have the musicians play something quiet, that you will eventually sing, and give everyone the chance to lower their friend into the house. If you have a big group, it will take some time. You might want some of your helpers to keep their eyes open for people who are sad or maybe need someone to pray with them for their friend.

When everyone is finished, sing some quiet songs asking our friend Jesus to help our other friends.

Finish with a prayer thanking Jesus for being our friend at all times.

As you say goodbye to everyone at the close of this service, you can suggest that they invite their friend to come along to church the following week or to the next all-age service.

SCRIPT

 Surprise and friends

 This is my friend

 Part 1: The wrecked roof (Mark 2:1)

Daniel dropped his stick sword and cringed when he heard his father's angry call.

'He must know about the broken pots,' Daniel said to himself.

There was nothing for a make-believe soldier to do but surrender, so he lowered his head in defeat and marched into the house.

It was a beautiful house. The best on the street. Daniel's father had built it himself. And many more houses in Capernaum too. Daniel's father was a good builder. But Daniel only seemed to be good at knocking things down.

'You broke three of your mother's best pots today,' said Daniel's father. 'What were you doing?'

'Saving our land from the Roman invaders, Father.'

Daniel's father cocked his head to one side and squinted at his son. It was the same look he gave a new wall, to make sure he'd built it straight. 'What?'

'Me and Reuben were the freedom fighters, and Adam and Josh were the Romans. We had them on the run! Then I swung my sword one last time and it sort of slipped out of my hand and flew across the room. . .'

'And crashed into your mother's pots.'

'Something like that,' said Daniel sheepishly. Then he raised his head and gave his father 'the look'. The look that said, 'I'm sorry and I'll try not to do it again, but I probably will, so won't you forgive me anyway and try not to be too angry, pleeeease?'

Daniel's father sighed. He had seen 'the look' the week before, when Daniel had scratched the front door.

And the week before that, when Daniel had knocked the dishes off the table.

And the week before that. . .

'That look won't work this time, son,' he said, as sternly as he could. 'Every afternoon for the next week, you will come to my workshop. You will put away the tools and sweep the floor, and you will not leave until the place is clean and tidy. It's about time you learned to fix things instead of tearing them up.'

Then Daniel's father turned around and marched out of the house.

Daniel stood there for a moment, staring at the floor. He scratched his head. He was puzzled. 'The look' was supposed to work.

Daniel's mother put her hand on his shoulder. 'Your father has a lot on his mind,' she said gently. 'His work, taking care of this house, his sick friend. . . and, besides, we have told you not to play that fighting game indoors.'

The next day, Daniel played with his friends for all he was worth. He knew that the playing would have to stop early all week. He couldn't forget this, and when the time finally came for him to go to the workshop, it was almost a relief.

It was even more of a relief when Daniel got to the workshop and found no one there. Well, a relief and a puzzle.

'Where is everybody?' he wondered.

And that's when Daniel heard the shouting. He ran outside and saw an excited crowd flooding into the street.

'What's happening?' yelled Daniel. 'Where are you going?'

'To the house of Aaron the Pharisee,' called back a young man.

'And he's making sick people well!' hollered an old blind woman, holding tight to the arm of her friend.

'Aaron the Pharisee's house?' thought Daniel. 'I know where that is. Father finished building it just last month.'

Daniel turned and called into the empty workshop, 'Does anyone here mind if I go and see what's happening at Aaron's house?'

Then he jumped into the crowd, which rushed like a wave to the Pharisee's door.

Did you hear anything in this story about a friend?

That's right – Daniel played with his friends. And Daniel's father was worried about his sick friend.

Were there other sick people in the story?

That's right – they were going to Aaron the Pharisee's house, because Jesus was there.

 Wanting to be in the presence of Jesus

Why don't we ask Jesus to come and be here with us as well!

 Thank Jesus for his presence

Part 2: The wrecked roof (Mark 2:2–12)

Unfortunately, by the time Daniel got to Aaron's house, it was already flooded with folk, and there was no room left inside.

Well, no room for most people. Daniel just dropped to all fours and crawled through the crowd as if they were the enemy line.

He scooted between legs.

He wriggled through gaps.

He used his make-believe sword once or twice.

And finally he was there, smack in the middle of Aaron's house – not a stick sword's length from Jesus.

Daniel had never seen anything like it. There was that old blind woman he'd seen on the street. She groped her way to Jesus, her hands stretched out in front of her so she wouldn't bump into anything.

Jesus took her hands and placed them at her side. Then he laid his own hands on those old blind eyes, bowed his head and prayed. And when he took his hands away, the woman's eyes shone clear, bright and blue.

The woman blinked once, blinked twice and then shouted, 'I can see! I can see!' louder and louder, over and over again.

She shouted for so long, Daniel put his hands over his ears.

She shouted so loud, Daniel thought she would shout the roof off the place.

And so she did.

Or so it seemed. Bits and pieces of stuff started to fall from the roof. The old woman laughed and pointed. She was just happy to be able to see it.

But all Daniel could think about was his father, who had put that roof up and would be anything but pleased to see it coming down.

The pieces were getting bigger, and it was clear that the woman's shouting had nothing to do with it. Someone was wrecking the roof!

Jesus stepped back.

Aaron the Pharisee stepped forward.

And the once-blind woman stepped out of the way.

Everyone else looked up at the roof. There were holes now, and hands – pairs of hands reaching through the holes to tear away those brand new tiles and make one great hole out of many.

All Daniel could think about was what his father would say. And how his father would look – red-faced, with his teeth clenched and his eyes dark, sharp slits.

And then Daniel saw his father.

But he wasn't in the crowd. He wasn't leaning through a window. He was up there – peering down through the hole in the roof. Daniel's father was wrecking his own roof!

And the look on his face was surprising. It wasn't the angry look Daniel had imagined. No, it was 'the look' – Daniel's look. And it was aimed at one furious Pharisee.

'Now, Aaron,' Daniel heard his father say, 'I know I just put this roof on. But one of my men has been sick, and the sickness left him paralysed. We tried to get in past the crowd, but we couldn't. And he needs to get in. He needs to see Jesus. This just seemed to be the most. . . practical way.'

And then he added, in a perfect Daniel tone, 'I'm sorry. I'll fix it. Free of charge.'

Aaron grunted his approval, and Daniel's father and three of his friends lowered a man down to Jesus on a bed with strong ropes at each corner.

What did Jesus do? Not what Daniel expected, that's for sure. Or anyone else either.

Jesus looked down at the man and said very clearly, 'Friend, your sins are forgiven.'

And Aaron the Pharisee stopped his grunting and started shouting.

'How dare you!' he roared at Jesus. 'And who do you think you are? Only God can forgive sins!'

'Hearts? Legs?' grinned Jesus. 'I suppose they are both pretty difficult to fix. So I'll fix one to prove that I can fix the other.'

Then he said to the man on the mat, 'Get up and walk.'

And he did!

So well, in fact, that he rolled up his own bed.

So well, he could have climbed back out of that hole if he'd wanted to.

But he walked through the crowd instead, praising God, with Daniel whooping and hollering behind.

'Daniel!' called a voice from the roof. 'What are you doing here?'

Oops. Daniel had forgotten about cleaning up the workshop.

Oh, well. He lowered his head and marched outside to meet his father.

Daniel's father was wiping his hands and grinning. 'Good work is important,' he said, 'but good friends are more important still.'

'So I can go and play with my friends now, instead of cleaning up your workshop?' asked Daniel, trying out 'the look' one last time.

> 'No,' his father answered slowly. 'I have to take care of the mess I made today, and you still have to clean the workshop.'
>
> Then Daniel's father picked him up and popped him on his shoulders.
>
> 'But after we've finished,' he said, 'I don't see any reason why you and I shouldn't both spend some time with our friends.'
>
> Daniel pulled out his stick sword and swung it around his head.
>
> 'Charge!' he shouted, and Daniel and his father galloped together all the way home.

 Jesus wants to be our friend

Many years before Jesus was born, a prophet called Isaiah said Jesus' wounds, the hurt he suffered on the cross, would take away the pain of all the bad things that happen to us and the bad things we do – our sickness and our sin. And that's just what Jesus did for the man who was lowered through the roof: he fixed all that was wrong with him.

Jesus himself said that there's no greater thing that someone can do than give his life for his friend. Jesus did that for us, on the cross. He wants to be our friend. And he wants to take care of our friends as well.

 Our friends' needs

Now, as the music is playing, we're going to bring our friends up to this house – this house with no roof, just like the one Daniel's dad made. And as we bring them up, you might want to pray for them. Perhaps your friend is having trouble, or is sick, or just needs to know that Jesus wants to be his or her friend too. So pray whatever you like for your friend, and then lower your friend into the house, like Daniel's dad lowered his friend (we'll be here to help you!) and set him before Jesus.

 Jesus, please help our friends

 Thank Jesus for being our friend

THE FEEDING OF THE FIVE THOUSAND

In advance

Prepare surprise bags for everyone: paper bags containing a pen, a fish-shaped piece of paper, a wrapped biscuit or cake, and stapled closed. Find a costume and/or actor for Huldah, and a 'belcher'!

Outline

1st Surprise bags

Praise God for his generosity and creativity

Thank God for his generosity and creativity

Part 1: The feeding of the five thousand (John 6:2)

My gift

Thank you, God, for my gift

Part 2: The feeding of the five thousand (John 6:2–14)

Praise God for his generosity

Use our gifts to serve God

Giving our gifts

Giving our lives for God's service

Thank God for our gifts

1st   I love surprise bags. We used to play a party game when I was a kid called 'the crying game'. Everyone would get three or four playing cards and when your card was drawn, you could pick something from the tray in the middle of the room. Most of these prizes were unwrapped – sweets, small toys, pens, bags of crisps, that sort of thing. But in the middle of the tray sat the untimate prize: the surprise bag. Experience had taught us that the surprise bag was far more desirable than anything else on the tray – even though what it contained was a mystery. Everyone wanted the surprise bag, and because of the way the crying game was designed, everyone quite literally had the chance to possess it – if only for a moment or two. You see, there were far fewer prizes than cards. And when the prizes on the tray ran out and your card was drawn, you could take a prize from someone else. Thus the name of the game. And thus the phenomenal amount of money my siblings and I have spent in counselling over the years!

Hopefully there will be no crying in this all-age service. But there will be surprise bags. Lots of them. Enough for one each. And perhaps, together, we can banish the ghosts of my ever-so-slightly disturbed childhood!

So what do you need? Lots and lots of little brown paper bags for a start, or any kind of small bag that you can't see through. You'll need one for each person (that's right – adults, children, everyone) that will be coming to the service and a few more for good measure. Into each bag you will place:

(a) a crayon, a pen or a marker, or some other form of writing implement
(b) a piece of paper cut in the shape of a fish
(c) a bun, a biscuit or some other kind of baked produce, preferably
       wrapped in clingfilm.

Having filled the bags, fold the top of each bag over on itself and then staple the top, so that they cannot be too easily opened.

Once everyone has been seated, have your volunteers give a bag to each person, with the instructions that the bags are not to be opened until you say so. You could give them out as people enter the room, but that is a more drawn-out process and the possibility of premature opening is greatly increased. Do this only if everyone in your church is possessed with a complete lack of curiosity.

Tell everyone that they have each been given a gift. A surprise gift. Tell them that God gives us gifts as well. Some are obvious and we can look at the world he made and see them: beautiful sunsets, towering mountains, amazing and extraordinary creatures. But some are not so obvious and they are hidden away inside each of us, amazing potential just waiting to be discovered and released. Just like the surprises in these bags. Just like the story we are about to hear.

Sing a few songs thanking God for his generosity, praising him for his creativity and celebrating the surprise he has placed in each of us.

And then offer him a simple prayer of thanks as well.

There are a couple of ways you could tell the story in the Story Box on page 93. You could simply do it on your own, bringing Huldah to life as you speak her lines and maybe even act out her huffing, puffing, determined walk. You could dress up as Huldah, with a robe and an apron and a tea towel head-dress. This will be particularly interesting if you are a guy. Or you could work together with a woman who is good at acting out, at miming, Huldah's actions. This will take some practice ahead of time, but there are no lines for her to say, which makes it easier. You will do all the lines as the narrator. She simply has to act out the part. With that in mind, it would probably be best if she was in costume (see tea towel, etc. above).

You should get the audience involved in the story as well – they have a very special part to play. Divide everyone into three groups: the left, the middle and the right of the room. Start with the group on your left and tell them to act shovelling food into their mouths and have them make a 'gobbling up' sound as they do it. Have them do it forcefully, but not too loud. Have the middle group do the same thing, but louder. And have the group on your right do it loudest of all. Then practise with the groups doing it in succession:

Left group: gobbling sound
Middle group: Gobbling Sound
Right group: GOBBLING SOUND

And then, for the *coup de grâce*, find someone in your group who is blessed with the very special gift of belching on demand. Hey, we're talking talents here, aren't we? And, trust me, there is someone (probably more than one someone) in your group who can do this. Speaking of surprises, the best volunteer I have ever had was a rather demure young lady. So don't just look to the boys!

If you are at all concerned that you will not be able to find someone 'on the spot', then by all means organise your belcher ahead of time. But you will still want to make a big song and dance about needing someone with a special God-given talent before you introduce that volunteer.

The belch comes in at the end of the three successive 'gobbling up' sounds. So it's:

Left group: gobbling sound
Middle group: Gobbling Sound
Right group: GOBBLING SOUND
BELCH!

This punctuates the activity and also gives your belcher sufficient time to 'work one up'! And you will probably want to 'mike' the belch as well, for maximum effect!

Practise this gobbling, belching sequence once or twice before the story begins.

Now start the story.

Pause and say that Huldah had a special gift: a gift for baking bread. Hulda had a secret recipe too. So now we are going to open our surprise bags and discover our secret gifts as well. Count to three and then tell them to open their bags and look inside. Open a bag from the front to demonstrate.

Ask everyone to take the paper fish and the crayon/pen out of the bag first and to leave the bun/biscuit alone and wrapped. Then ask them to write whatever gift or talent they believe God has given them on the fish. It might even be helpful to have them work in little groups on this, so others can make suggestions if someone gets stuck. Tell them that this is no time for humility. We want them to be honest about what God has given them.

When everyone has done this, ask the group for a couple of suggestions.

Lead everyone in a simple prayer: 'Thank you, God, for giving me the gift of. . .' and everyone fills in the blank out loud with whatever gift they have.

Continue the story from page 94.

As soon as the story is finished, move right into another song about God's generosity. Something really 'up' and exciting, I think.

After the song, say something like this: 'When God made the world, he made it good. And one of the good things he did was to make man and woman, and he gave them gifts and he gave them work to do and he made them happy with who they were. Happy with themselves. That's why they didn't mind being naked. They weren't ashamed of themselves. When man and woman disobeyed God, suddenly they were ashamed, not just of what they'd done but of who they were.

'When Jesus came, he came to turn that bad thing good again; to celebrate our gifts – whatever it is we have to bring to him, like the boy brought his loaves and fishes. Like Huldah used her bread-making talent.

'God wants us to be happy with what he has given us – our talents and our abilities. But he wants us to do something else with them as well. He wants us to use them to help one another.

'That's what Nathan and Huldah did, wasn't it? Even though she didn't know it at the time. And he wants us to do the same. Because when he made the world, God made something else good: man's relationship with the person next to him. He made me special and you too. And he wants me to treat you as though you're special and to use my gifts to serve and help you. That's another thing that Jesus came to make good again. Something that was lost when Adam and Eve disobeyed God and then blamed each other.'

'So here's what I want each of you to do. Put your fish with your talents on, and your crayon and your biscuit (if you've taken it out), back into the bag, and then get up and walk around the room and give your surprise bag to someone else. And when you do it, say something like, "This is my talent. God gave it to me and I want to thank him by giving it to you." '

Then play some quiet music while everyone mills around giving their surprises away to each other. Maybe some will pray together.

When it looks as if things are settling down, lead everyone in a quieter song about serving others or giving our lives for God's service.

 Then finish with a prayer – a prayer of thanks for our gifts again, and for the lovely biscuits or cakes.

And when the prayer is finished, tell them they can gobble up their cakes for real. Hooray! Or maybe BELCH!

SCRIPT

 Surprise bags

You have each been given a gift. A surprise gift. God gives us gifts as well. Some are obvious and we can look at the world he made and see them: beautiful sunsets, towering mountains, amazing and extraordinary creatures. But some are not so obvious and they are hidden away inside each of us, amazing potential just waiting to be discovered and released. Just like the surprises in these bags. Just like the story we are about to hear today.

 Praise God for his generosity and creativity

 Thank God for his generosity and creativity

 Part 1: The feeding of the five thousand (John 6:2)

Left group: gobbling sound
Middle group: Gobbling Sound
Right group: GOBBLING SOUND
Belcher: BELCH!
Practise this gobbling, belching sequence once or twice before the story begins.

Huldah was a baker. The best baker in all Bethsaida. She baked cookies and cakes and pies, but her speciality was bread – barley bread – and people would come from all around just to gobble it down! (*Do gobbling, belching bit here*)
  Huldah had a secret recipe.
  She would pick the grain and grind it into flour.
  Sort the measures and mix in the water.
  And then bake it with just a little. . . well, that was Huldah's secret!

 My gift

Huldah had a special gift, a gift for baking bread. Hulda had a secret recipe too. So now we are going to open our surprise bags and discover our secret gifts as well.

I will count to three and then you may open your bag and look inside. One, two, three. . . *(Open a bag from the front to demonstrate)*

Take the paper fish and the crayon/pen out of the bag but leave the bun/biscuit alone and wrapped!

Write whatever gift or talent you believe God has given you on the fish. This is no time for humility – be honest about what God has given you!

 Thank you, God, for my gift

Thank you, God, for giving me the gift of. . . *(Everyone fills in the blank out loud)*

 Part 2: The feeding of the five thousand (John 6:2–14)

One day, when Huldah had finished her baking, she put away her bowls and her spoons. She swept her floor. She took off her apron. And she decided to take a walk – to the top of the hill that towered over Bethsaida.

A teacher named Jesus was up there, talking. And most of the town was there too, listening to what he had to say.

So Huldah huffed and puffed and puffed and huffed her way up the hill. It was getting late, and the higher she climbed, the lower the sun fell behind her, dropping its orange light into the lake below, and stretching her wide shadow until it was tall and thin.

When she reached the top, Huldah was exhausted. So she sucked in a big breath of air. And that's when she smelled it – the crusty aroma of freshly baked bread!

'Hmm,' Huldah thought. 'Where did that come from? How did that get here? I wonder – who brought the bread?'

Then Huldah saw the crowd, gathered in groups like bunches of grapes. Then Huldah heard the crowd, noisy and loud like a storm at sea. And what were they doing? They were gobbling down fish and bread. *(Do gobbling/belching action here)*

'Huldah!' came a voice from the nearest bunch. 'Have you tasted the bread? It's the best bread I've ever eaten!'

The voice belonged to Huldah's best friend, Joanna. But Huldah did not think her comment was very friendly at all.

'The best bread?' Huldah huffed. 'Certainly not the best bread. Surely my bread is the best bread you've ever eaten!'

'Oh, no,' Joanna insisted. 'This is the best bread – the best I've ever eaten!'

'But where did you get it?' asked Huldah. 'Where did it come from? Tell me, please. Who brought the bread?'

'I don't know,' Joanna shrugged. 'One of Jesus' friends gave it to me. He's standing over there. Why don't you go and ask him?' And she pointed to the other side of the hill. So Huldah huffed and puffed and puffed and huffed her way across the hill. And when she came to Jesus' friend, there were her relatives – her aunts and uncles and cousins – sitting on the ground around him. And they too were gobbling down fish and bread. (*Gobbling/belching action*)

'Huldah!' called her cousin, Caleb. 'Have you tasted the bread? It's the best bread I've ever eaten!'

Huldah was annoyed now.

'The best bread?' she grumbled. 'Certainly not the best bread. Surely my bread is the best bread you've ever eaten!'

'Oh, no,' insisted Caleb. 'This is the best bread – the best I've ever eaten!' And the others all chewed and nodded in agreement.

So Huldah picked up a piece. Sure enough, it was golden brown on the outside like hers. She tore it in half and sniffed again. Yes, it smelled like her bread. So she had to ask; she just had to ask. 'Where did it come from? How did it get here? Someone tell me, please. Who brought the bread?'

'I don't know,' answered Jesus' friend. 'Jesus gave it to me and asked me to pass it round. Why don't you ask him? He's right over there.' And he pointed to the other side of the hill – the side from which Huldah had just come.

So Huldah huffed and puffed and puffed and huffed her way back to the other side of the hill. And when she came to Jesus, who was sitting on the ground around him? Her own family! Her mother and father. Her husband and children. All gobbling down fish and bread. (*Gobbling/belching action*)

'Huldah!' called her father. 'Huldah, have you tasted the bread? This is the best bread I've ever eaten!' And then he added, 'Huldah, you've got to get the recipe!'

'Get the recipe?' cried Huldah. 'GET THE RECIPE? My bread is the best bread in all Bethsaida! I don't need another recipe!'

Then she grabbed a piece of the bread, tore off a chunk and popped it into her mouth. Like a wine-taster, she rolled it around her tongue. Then she chewed it up and swallowed it down. And as she did so, her eyes filled up with tears. For everyone was right. It was the best bread. The best she'd ever eaten!

'But where did it come from?' begged Huldah. 'How did it get here? Will someone tell me, please, who brought the bread?'

And that's when someone started to giggle – someone sitting in the middle of the crowd. Someone who looked a lot like Huldah's own son!

'Nathan!' shouted Huldah. 'What are you laughing about? There's nothing funny about this. Nothing at all.'

'It's your question, Mum. That's all. You see, we were sitting up here, listening to Jesus, when everybody got pretty hungry. Jesus sent his friends around to see if anyone had any food, and I said I had my packed lunch. You know – the one you packed me, with the fish and the bread. I knew it wouldn't go far but I gave it to Jesus anyway. Then he prayed and he broke it into pieces and he fed us with it. Thousands of us! Who brought the bread, Mum? It looks like you did!'

'But how?' asked Huldah. 'How did he do it? How did he make so much?'

'I don't know,' Nathan shrugged. 'Maybe Jesus has a secret recipe too!'

And that's when someone ran up to Jesus.

'Jesus!' he said. 'Jesus, can I have some more of that bread? It's the best bread I've ever eaten!'

So Jesus gave him some bread and he gobbled it down. (*Gobbling/belching action – one last time*)

And Huldah just smiled, a smile as warm and shiny as a freshly baked bun.

 Praise God for his generosity

 Use our gifts to serve God

When God made the world, he made it good. And one of the good things he did was to make man and woman, and he gave them gifts and he gave them work to do and he made them happy with who they were. Happy with themselves. That's why they didn't mind being naked. They weren't ashamed of themselves. When man and woman disobeyed God, suddenly they were ashamed, not just of what they'd done but of who they were. When Jesus came, he came to turn that bad thing good again. To celebrate our gifts – whatever it is we have to bring to him, like the boy brought his loaves and fishes. Like Huldah used her bread-making talent.

God wants us to be happy with what he has given us – our talents and our abilities. But he wants us to do something else with them as well. He wants us to use them to help one another.

That's what Nathan and Huldah did, wasn't it? Even though she didn't know it at the time. And he wants us to do the same. Because when he made the world, God made something else good: man's relationship with the person next to him. He made me special and you too. And he wants me to treat you as if you're special and to use my gifts to serve and help you. That's another thing that Jesus came to make good again. Something that was lost when Adam and Eve disobeyed God and then blamed each other.

 Giving our gifts

So here's what I want each of you to do. Put your fish with your talents on, and your crayon, and your biscuit (if you've taken it out), back into the bag, and then get up and walk around the room and give your surprise bag to someone else. And when you do it, say something like, 'This is my talent. God gave it to me and I want to thank him by giving it to you.'

 Giving our lives for God's service

 Thank God for our gifts

WALKING ON WATER

In advance

Set up your 'boat' at the front. If you decide to perform the story as a drama, cast the parts and rehearse.

Strips of brown paper; pens; Blu-tack.

Outline

'Row, row, row your boat'

On board

Part 1: Walking on water (John 6:16–17)

My fears

Part 2: Walking on water (John 6:18)

For sensitivity to others' fears

Part 3: Walking on water (John 6:19–21)

Jesus can take away our fears

Seeking Jesus

Jesus, help us when we're afraid

In God's new kingdom mankind will be in charge of nature again

The power and love of Jesus

🎵 Right then, let's begin this service with that famous worship song, 'Row, row, row your boat'! You'll need to do it as a round, of course. I mean, what other way is there? Dividing your group into three should work just fine. If you don't feel confident leading the singing or bringing the groups in at the right time, get someone else (or three someone elses – one for each group) to help you.

🔵 **1st** When the song is over, tell your group that today's story takes place on a boat, but that it is definitely not a 'merrily, merrily, merrily, merrily' experience for at least one of the passengers.

📖 You can tell the story in the Story Box on pages 102–3 in one of two ways. You can either do it yourself (or have someone else tell it) or you can get a group to act it out. As you will see, the way the story is constructed lends itself to a dramatic interpretation, but doing that will take a lot more preparation. It will need to be practised ahead of time, and lines (even though they are relatively few) will need to be memorised. The narrator could read her bit (holding a big book at the side), but if everyone else in the cast is fumbling with papers it doesn't work very well. It's clunky and not as much fun. It's one thing to lead a group in shouting out the odd line in a story – sometimes the mistakes make that even more enjoyable, because the gist of the tale is being told by someone who has already worked through it – but if you are attempting to do a drama, it needs to be done as well as possible. Just my opinion, but, hey, I'm writing the book!

Whether the story is acted or told, it is in three parts, stopping along the way to consider the meaning of the story.

So tell the first part now.

🤸 Matthew was afraid of being in the boat. The question for your group is, 'What are they afraid of?' You will need some kind of big boat shape up front. It could be the outline of a boat on big paper, Blu-tacked to a wall. It could be a big cardboard box that stands on its own with a boat shape drawn on it. It could even be a real boat, if you can borrow one. Have strips of brown paper that look like the planking on the side of a wooden boat and felt markers or crayons at different stations around the room. Invite everyone to write or draw something that they are afraid of on the plank-strips, and then attach the strips to the boat shape. If you have a real boat, forget about the plank-strip pieces of paper and just have them write or draw on regular paper – any colour will do – and then drop the papers into the boat.

Have your band play some music in the background, or play some recorded music quietly, while everyone does this.

When everyone has attached a 'fear' to the boat, read out a few. Don't ask who put them there. You don't want to embarrass anyone. But it might be helpful to follow each suggestion with 'Yes, lots of people are scared of that' and if you want, and it's true, you might even like to say, 'And me as well!' Maybe add a little story about when you found a spider in your bathtub – that sort of thing. The idea to get across is that, like Matthew, everyone is afraid of something.

Then say something like, 'So Matthew was afraid. Like we are all afraid of something. Let's see what happened next!'

As you tell the next part of the story (from page 103), you really need to get across the sense of Matthew's fear. You can do that with your voice or your actors, but you might also like to include everyone else by having them make whooshing wind noises and pretend that they are being tossed about in the boat.

Stop the story here and acknowledge that when we are frightened it doesn't help when people make fun of us, just because that's not the thing that frightens them. What might work even better is to have someone else stop you and make that point. Maybe they can say something like, 'I remember when I was afraid and no one else was and I felt just like Matthew.'

Ask everyone to bow their head, and pray that God will help you all to be more sensitive to each other when things are troubling you.

Now back to the story on page 104.

Now have another little talk – or get someone else to do it (another voice often helps concentration) – but keep it short. Say something like: 'What did we say? Some people are afraid of one thing; some people of another. Matthew was afraid of water. Peter was afraid of ghosts. But all the fear stopped when Jesus finally climbed aboard. It was their friend out there all along, and he took them safely on to the other shore.

'They were amazed all right. You can just imagine their jaws dropping to the floor when they realised that Jesus was walking on the water. But that's a different kind of "afraid" – an afraid that we call "awe" or "wonder". It's the kind of feeling we get when we see something huge and amazing, like an enormous mountain or a lightning strike or the northern lights.

'But their fear – that something bad would happen and they would have to face it alone and terrified – disappeared when Jesus climbed on board.'

Sing a few songs, probably quieter to mid-tempo songs, about seeing Jesus and him being near. Because when we see him, our fears can go away too.

At the end of the songs, have everyone bow their head and pray that Jesus would help them when they are afraid. You might even want to have everyone hold their hands in front of them, as though their fears are perched there, and then let those fears go as they pray. Or, if you have used something only slightly sticky to attach the planks to the boat, you could even have them walk up, as they feel led, take a plank from the boat (not even necessarily their plank – let's do this for each other) and tear that plank in half.

When the singing and the praying have finished ask them if they remember that when God made the world good, one of the good things he did was to put mankind in charge of nature. Then tell them that one of the reasons Jesus did his nature miracles (walking on water, stilling storms, turning water into wine) was to show that in God's kingdom, in the new heaven and new earth that God was bringing, mankind would be in charge of nature again.

Then finish your time together by singing one or two really boisterous songs about Jesus and his power and love.

SCRIPT

 'Row, row, row your boat'

 On board

Today's story takes place on a boat, but it is definitely not a 'merrily, merrily, merrily, merrily' experience for at least one of the passengers.

 Part 1: Walking on water (John 6:16–17)

'I'm not going!' Matthew insisted. 'And that's all there is to it.'

'But it's only a boat ride,' said James.

'And it's just across the lake,' added John.

'I think he's chicken,' sniggered Andrew.

'Buck-buck-buck,' clucked Peter.

'All right, I'm afraid. I admit it,' Matthew shrugged. 'And you're not. But that's only because you were fishermen before you met Jesus. You know I was a tax collector who'd spent all of his time on land. So it's no use poking fun at me. You've travelled in boats all your lives, but I can't even swim.'

'So what are you going to do?' asked Andrew. 'Jesus told us to meet him on the other side.'

'I'll wait and go with him,' said Matthew.

'And how do you suppose he'll get there?' asked Peter.

'Maybe he'll walk,' Matthew answered.

'What, along the shore?' snorted Peter. 'That would take ages. And he told us he'd see us in the morning.'

'Jesus will obviously have to travel in another boat,' James explained. 'Which means that if you wait for him, you'll end up in a boat anyway. So why not come with us?'

Matthew sighed. James had a point – they all did – and there was no use arguing any longer.

'All right,' he agreed at last. 'But try to keep it smooth.'

'Keep it smooth?' Peter chuckled to Andrew. 'He's definitely never been on a boat before!' Matthew hiked up his robes and stepped gingerly from the shore into the boat. It rocked, ever so gently, but that was enough to send him trembling to the floor, planting his bottom firmly on the nearest seat and hanging on to the side for dear life.

Some more of Jesus' friends followed. But the four fishermen plunged straight into the lake. They pushed out the boat until it was fully afloat, and hopped in, soaking wet, beside their frightened friend.

'See?' said Peter, slapping Matthew on the back with a big wet hand. 'Safe as houses!'

'Yeah,' Matthew muttered. 'Soggy, drippy houses.'

And the four fishermen just laughed and started to row.

 My fears

Matthew was afraid of being in the boat. What are you afraid of?

Do activity

So Matthew was afraid. Like we are all afraid of something. Let's see what happened next!

 Part 2: Walking on water (John 6:18)

Matthew watched the sky grow dark and the shoreline slowly disappear. He was trying to look calm, but inside his head a voice was shouting, 'What if we tip over? What if I fall out? Let's go back. Let's go back now! Turn the boat around! Please!'

He knew that wasn't going to happen, of course. Not while the others were laughing and talking and having such a good time. And, besides, he didn't want them making fun of him any more.

'Enjoying the ride?' asked James.

'Not so bad, is it?' added John.

'I think he's going to be sick!' sniggered Andrew.

And Peter just laughed and made the most disgusting noise.

'No, I'm fine. Just fine,' Matthew said, forcing a weak smile.

But he wasn't fine for long.

The wind began to blow and the choppy waves that followed tossed the little boat up and down on the lake.

Matthew shut his eyes and held on even tighter. That voice in his head was screaming now.

And Matthew was about to scream as well, when a big wave washed into the boat and knocked him clean off his seat and onto the floor.

 For sensitivity to others' fears

 Part 3: Walking on water (John 6:19–21)

Matthew opened his eyes, searching for something to hang on to. He was soaking wet. So were his friends. And the sky and the sea looked like some great dark beast intent on swallowing them all.

'Surely,' he thought, 'the fishermen will be frightened now.'

But no, they were talking and rowing and remembering storms they had sailed through in days gone by.

'This is nothing compared to the one we got caught in two years ago,' shouted James.

'Twenty-foot waves!' added John.

'We thought we'd had it, didn't we, Peter?' called Andrew.

But Peter said nothing. He didn't laugh. He didn't chuckle. He didn't joke. And he had stopped rowing altogether.

'What's the matter?' asked James.

'There's something out there,' said Peter. 'Something on the water.' And the wind whipped his trembling words right round the boat.

'Something out there?' shouted James. 'You're having us on! Come on, Peter, let it go. Poor Matthew is already terrified. Leave him alone.'

'I'm not joking!' Peter shouted back. And his voice sounded terrified too. 'There's something out there – something I've never seen before.'

The others peered into the darkness, but darkness was all they could see.

'Maybe it was a flash of lightning. Or a gull. Or another boat,' suggested John.

'I've seen lightning. I've seen gulls. I've seen boats,' shouted Peter, and his fear was mixed with anger now. 'But that's not what's out there.'

And then the lightning really did flash. And everyone screamed. Because everyone saw it: a tall white figure walking through the waves.

'It's a ghost!' shouted James.

'An evil spirit, surely!' added John.

'It's coming straight for us!' cried Andrew.

'We've got to get out of here!' yelled Peter. And he grabbed his oar and pulled with all his might.

But no matter how hard the fishermen rowed, the ghost on the water kept up with the boat.

The lightning flashed and tracked its ghoulish course. It looked as if there was nothing they could do to escape.

And that's when Matthew cried, 'Stop!' But now his voice did not sound at all frightened or terrified.

'Are you mad?' shouted James.

'Crackers!' added John.

'Keep rowing!' Andrew ordered.

And Peter just pulled and grunted.

'No, I mean it,' said Matthew. 'Stop! I know who it is. It's Jesus!'

'You're not a chicken,' growled Peter. 'You're a loon. What would Jesus be doing in the middle of the lake? How would he get here? And that thing is walking – it's walking on the water. How would Jesus do that?'

'I don't know,' answered Matthew. 'But I do know what I see. You were fishermen. I was a tax collector. And the one thing that every tax collector knows is how to tell what's real from what's not. Real coins from fake ones. Real accounts from phoney ones. And I'm telling you: that's Jesus out there.'

Peter turned around – the ghostly figure was walking straight towards him. The fisherman trembled. He shivered. He shook.

And then the figure spoke: 'Hello, everybody. There's no need to be afraid. It's just me. Thought I'd catch up with you. Mind if I come aboard?'

Matthew was right. It was Jesus. It really was.

So they helped him into the boat. And as soon as they did, the wind died down, the sea was calm again and in a flash they were at the other side of the lake.

'Thank goodness for that!' sighed Matthew. 'I don't think I could have spent another minute in that boat.'

And this time nobody sniggered and nobody laughed. But nobody was afraid any more either.

> The fishermen just stared at Jesus, shocked and surprised, and gave thanks to God for their amazing water-walking friend.
>
> _Storytelling options:_
> _You can use the 'stilling of the storm' story instead of this one, if you like. There is a very nice retelling in my_ Storyteller Bible.

? Jesus can take away our fears

What did we say? Some people are afraid of one thing; some people of another. Matthew was afraid of water. Peter was afraid of ghosts. But all the fear stopped when Jesus finally climbed aboard. It was their friend out there all along, and he took them safely on to the other shore.

They were amazed all right. You can just imagine their jaws dropping to the floor when they realised that Jesus was walking on the water. But that's a different kind of 'afraid' – an afraid that we call 'awe' or 'wonder'. It's the kind of feeling we get when we see something huge and amazing, like an enormous mountain or a lightning strike or the northern lights.

But their fear – that something bad would happen and they would have to face it alone and terrified – disappeared when Jesus climbed on board.

 _Seeking Jesus_

Jesus, help us when we're afraid

? In God's new kingdom mankind will be in charge of nature again

Do you remember that when God made the world good, one of the good things he did was to put mankind in charge of nature? One of the reasons Jesus did his nature miracles (walking on water, stilling storms, turning water into wine) was to show that in God's kingdom, in the new heaven and new earth that God was bringing, mankind would be in charge of nature again.

 The power and love of Jesus

RESURRECTION

In advance

Cast the radio play and rehearse. Set out four lecterns/music stands.

Outline

1st Radio intro

🎵 Resurrection celebration

☑ Part 1: Resurrection (Luke 24:13–29)

🤸 Grapes and feelings

🎵 Resurrection

☑ Part 2: Resurrection (Luke 24:29–35)

❓ After the firstfruit

🔥 Thank God for resurrection

🎵 Thank God for resurrection

1st We've told our stories in lots of different ways, haven't we? For the resurrection, we're going to do something extra special. We're going to do a radio play. You will need four voices or, more precisely, four volunteers to stand up front and read their parts with enthusiasm. Ideally, it would be helpful for them to practise this, because the humour in the stories is very much dependent on the timing.

You will need a narrator, Jesus, Mr Cleopas and Mrs Cleopas. As I wrote the story, I heard Mr Cleopas with a strong regional accent: Yorkshire, Lancashire or maybe Somerset. Mrs Cleopas struck me as more of the Hyacinth Bucket type – faux posh, if you know what I mean. I think a guy doing her with one of those Monty Python/*Little Britain* 'Laaaydeee' voices would also be fantastic – particularly as the group will be watching.

Set four lecterns/music stands in a row up front. You want Mr and Mrs Cleopas next to each other, Jesus next to them and then the narrator. Everyone should be at their places when the service begins, then you can introduce the play by saying something like, 'And now really live from the studios of Station NOTDEAD, the tale of Mr and Mrs Cleopas and the Mysterious Stranger' (followed by a 'woo-oo-oo' from your cast). Ham it up – that's the point. Enjoy this and everyone else will too.

Then add, 'This programme is brought to you by Firstfruits Limited, purveyors of fine homegrown apples, oranges and melons. Why eat the leftovers when you can have the firstfruits? But before we begin, a little musical number.'

Get everyone on their feet and have them provide that musical number (or even two). Something big and boisterous, celebrating the resurrection.

Go straight into the first part of the play, in the Story Box on pages 111–14.

Then have an announcer (it can be the narrator) say, 'As a special Easter promotion, our sponsor, Firstfruits Limited, would like you to sample some of their wares. So have a grape or two, and when you do you'll know the answer too – why eat the leftovers when you can have the firstfruits?'

Have some volunteers pass around seedless grapes. And while everyone is munching, ask them to find a partner and share two things: how it feels when someone you love dies, and what it might feel like if someone told you they were alive again. Then take a few answers to each of the questions.

Sing another, quieter song about the resurrection, and then get back to the show.

Conclude the story from page 114.

Now pick up a bunch of grapes (you might need to have set one aside) and say to the group, 'Do you know why our show was sponsored by Firstfruits Limited? It's because, in his letter to the Corinthians, the apostle Paul says that Jesus is the firstfruits of the resurrection. The firstfruits are the ones that are on the tree first, when the harvest starts to come in. So if you look at a tree and there are a few apples on it, you can be pretty sure that more apples will follow. And the same with grapes or oranges. The firstfruits show us what's coming next. So if Jesus is the firstfruits of the resurrection, then we can find out what will happen to us when we are resurrected by looking at what happened to him.

'Was there anything about Jesus after he was resurrected that was the same as before he died and was resurrected?' (Might want to take a few answers here.) 'Sure, he could walk and talk. He could pick up things. He broke bread. He wasn't like a ghost.

'But were there things that were different? Yes again. He could appear and disappear, just like that. And sometimes he looked like himself, so his friends could recognise him, and sometimes he didn't.

'But the key thing is that his new, resurrected body would never die again – it was his for ever. And in the same way, God will give us a resurrected body: a body that will live for ever. And it will be the same in some ways, but in other ways it will be different. Just like Jesus. For we are the fruit that follows the firstfruit.

'And even more amazing than that, God is going to resurrect our whole world – make a new heaven and a new earth – and just like our bodies, some of it will be old and familiar (the best bits, I think) and some of it will be new and transformed and built to last for ever.'

If you feel you need to make the idea of firstfruits clearer – and let's face it, most of us don't live in agricultural settings – it might be helpful to project images of a branch with blossoms, then one or two bits of fruit, and then branches full of the same fruit.

'So let's bow our heads and thank God for the resurrection: for Jesus, the first-fruits, and for our resurrection and the resurrection of those we love and miss. And for the promise of a new heaven and a new earth one day, where we can share in God's great feast for ever.'

 So pray. . .

 . . .and sing again – big and loud, I think – thanking God for resurrection.

Options:
The advantage to the radio play format is that no one has to memorise lines. They just need to deliver them well. But if you'd like another approach, you have a couple of options. You could simply do these as live dramas, but there will need to be a lot more rehearsal time. Or you could make a short film of Mr and Mrs Cleopas. It would be terrific fun, and these days, with the ready availability of digital cameras and film-making technology (I've got a perfectly

good program for doing that on the MacBook I'm using now), it's relatively easy. But, again, it would require a lot of time. It might be worth it though, as I think that budding film-makers are an underused bunch as far as church and communication go, and you might just have that talent in your congregation, waiting to be released.

And finally, if you have enjoyed Mr and Mrs Cleopas, there are two more sketches that fit between the ones I have included (and adapted) here. They were originally written for *The Big Start* at Spring Harvest 2008, and in case you were there and would like to use the other two, I thought it would only be fair to include them in this chapter as well. I don't think that there would be time to do all four in one service (and that's why I have edited together the two that I thought best summarised our Easter hope), but you might want to use them another time. So they are in Story Boxes on pages 118–21 and 121–24.

SCRIPT

 Radio intro

And now really live from the studios of Station NOTDEAD, the tale of Mr and Mrs Cleopas and the Mysterious Stranger. (*'Woo-oo-oo' from your cast*)

This programme is brought to you by Firstfruits Limited, purveyors of fine homegrown apples, oranges and melons. Why eat the leftovers when you can have the firstfruits? But before we begin, a little musical number.

 Resurrection celebration

 Part 1: Resurrection (Luke 24:13–29)

Three days after Jesus died, he came back to earth from the dead. And when he did, he had a brand new back-from-the-dead kind of body.

This was, in some ways, very helpful. He could walk through locked doors and appear suddenly to his friends out of nowhere.

But in other ways it wasn't helpful at all. For his brand new body was different enough from his old one that even his friends didn't always recognise him at first. And he was mistaken for gardeners and ghosts and all sorts.

This is pretty much what happened when he bumped into his friends, Mr and Mrs Cleopas. They were walking back from Jerusalem, where they'd been staying, to their little country house in Emmaus. And they were very unhappy.

'Ah, Mrs Cleopas,' sighed Mr Cleopas. 'It's hopeless times we're living in. Our friend Jesus is put to death and now, just three days later, the rumours. Tomb empty. Body stolen. And all this talk of rising from the dead.'

'Why can't they just let the poor man rest in peace?' sniffled Mrs Cleopas. And then she added, 'Mr Cleopas, the tissues please.'

So Mr Cleopas. . . passed her the tissues.

'There you go, duck.'

And that's when Jesus appeared, right out of nowhere and right beside them!

'So, what are you talking about?' he asked.

'You must be the only fella in the whole of Jerusalem who hasn't heard,' sighed Mr Cleopas.

'It's what happened to Jesus.'

These friends didn't recognise him either. So Jesus decided to have a little fun. 'And what was that?' he asked, trying very hard not to smile.

'Mr Cleopas, the information, please,' said Mrs Cleopas.

But it was all Mr Cleopas could do to tell the tale without his wife's help. 'Well, it were like this. . .' he began.

'Jesus of Nazareth was a prophet,' interrupted Mrs Cleopas. 'Blessed by God. Loved by the people. Powerful in all he said and did.'

'That's right,' nodded Mr Cleopas. 'And then. . .'

'And then, in spite of all he'd done,' cried Mrs Cleopas, 'our religious leaders handed him over to the Romans, who crucified him. The very one we thought might be the Messiah, God's Chosen One, our only hope for freedom.'

'Exactly,' noted Mr Cleopas. 'But now three days have passed. . .'

'Passed, Mr Cleopas! Three days, passed!' wailed Mrs Cleopas. 'And now some of our lady friends say that his tomb is empty, his body gone, and that an angel has told them he is alive! It's just all too much to take in.'

Jesus had a little think. This had started out as a bit of fun, but perhaps he could use the situation to help his friends understand what his death and resurrection was all about. 'I believe that Moses and the prophets have a thing or two to say about this,' Jesus began.

'Moses and the prophets!' exclaimed Mrs Cleopas. 'We have just the thing. Mr Cleopas, the portable Scripture scrolls, please.'

Mr Cleopas fished around in his big travelling bag. 'I were thinking the same thing, duck.' And he pulled out a box filled with tiny scrolls and passed it over to Jesus.

Jesus opened the box, pulled out a scroll and unrolled it.

'This is remarkable,' he said. 'The book of Exodus, yes?'

'That's right,' grinned Mr Cleopas. 'It's small, but it's all there. Manufactured by a company called Judges Inc. Descendants of Gideon, if I'm not mistaken.'

'And what are these letters in red?'

'The words of the Lord God himself,' said Mr Cleopas. 'Makes them easier to pick out.'

'I'll have to remember that,' said Jesus. 'So where do you get these?'

'Well, all sorts of places,' muttered Mr Cleopas, suddenly looking rather sheepish. 'Shops, markets, umm. . .'

'The Ramallah Inn?' asked Jesus, examining the bottom of the box.

'Yes, well, hmm,' Mr Cleopas stammered. 'Wonder how that got in there.'

Meanwhile, Mrs Cleopas was looking equally sheepish.

'Mr Cleopas, the towels,' she whispered. 'The towels.'

'Right then, duck.' And he passed her two white towels that were in the bag as well.

'Hang on!' said Jesus. 'Those say "Property of the Ramallah Inn" as well!'

'Did I say "Pass the towels", Mr Cleopas?' grumbled Mrs Cleopas.

'I believe you did, duck.'

'I did not. It was a simple and subtle warning in the hope that you might keep the towels hidden.'

'Sorry, duck, I could have sworn that you said "Pass. . ." '

'Never mind,' Jesus interrupted. 'The white woolly towels have given me an idea. Is the book of the prophet Isaiah in here anywhere? I think the passage I'm looking for is in the middle.'

Then he unrolled the scroll and had a quick read.

'Ah yes, here it is. Listen:'

"He was despised and rejected by men,
a man of sorrows, and familiar with suffering.
Like one from whom men hide their faces
he was despised, and we esteemed him not."

'Does this sound like your friend who died?'

'It does, sir,' nodded Mr Cleopas. 'It does indeed.'

'That's what I thought,' said Jesus. 'And now it says why he had to suffer. Listen:

"Surely he took up our infirmities
and carried our sorrows. . .
the punishment that brought us peace was upon him,
and by his wounds we are healed."

'And now here's the white woolly bit:

"We all, like sheep, have gone astray,
each of us has turned to his own way;

and the Lord has laid on him
the iniquity of us all."

'Don't you see?' said Jesus. 'Your friend died to set you free – not from the Romans but from all the bad things you have ever done. And there's plenty of hope in that! Hope in Jesus and what he did on the cross.'

'But what about all these rumours?' asked Mrs Cleopas. 'The missing body? The empty tomb?'

'That's in here as well,' grinned Jesus. 'Just a little further along:

"After the suffering of his soul,
he will see the light of life and be satisfied."

'He will see the light of life!' Jesus repeated. 'Even more hope. So perhaps these rumours are true. Perhaps your friend really has come back to life again, just as the prophet said.'

'Hope and more hope!' exclaimed Mrs Cleopas. 'All because of Jesus. Ah, Strange and Sudden Travelling Companion, you have been such a help. We're almost home. Won't you stop and have supper with us?'

'I'd be delighted,' said Jesus. 'It will give me time to tell you just one or two more things about hope.'

 Grapes and feelings

As a special Easter promotion, our sponsor, Firstfruits Limited, would like you to sample some of their wares. So have a grape or two, and when you do, you'll know the answer too. Why eat the leftovers when you can have the firstfruits?

 Resurrection

 Part 2: Resurrection (Luke 24:29–35)

'It's getting dark,' said Mr Cleopas. 'And there's robbers and beasties and all sorts out there.

Why don't you stay the night?'

'I'd love to,' said Jesus. 'But I really need to keep going.'

'At this hour?' said Mrs Cleopas. 'Nonsense. No, you're staying with us, Kind and Hopefully Not an Axe-Murdering Stranger. Mr Cleopas, the front door key, please.'

So Mr Cleopas reached into his big travelling bag and passed his wife the key.

'Now then,' said Mrs Cleopas, once they had sat themselves down. 'How's about I whip up a little something for tea?'

'That would be lovely,' said Jesus.

But Mr Cleopas looked suddenly uncomfortable. Very uncomfortable indeed.

'I've got a better idea,' he said. 'Why don't we give this nice young fella some of that lovely fresh bread we picked up at the shop on the way? You know – the place we stopped at before he suddenly and quite unexpectedly appeared. It would just save you the bother, that's all, duck. Get you off your feet.'

'That's fine with me,' said Jesus. 'I don't want you going to any trouble.'

'No trouble at all,' said Mrs Cleopas, glaring at Mr Cleopas. 'It's just that my husband has got it into his head that I'm not a very good cook. Isn't that right, Mr Cleopas?'

'It's not that, duck,' stammered Mr Cleopas. 'It's just that. . .'

'It's just that you are a fussy eater, Mr Cleopas! I blame your mother, I do. Cutting the crusts off your sandwiches. Letting you leave those lovely sprouts on your plate. I'm sure our guest will be perfectly happy with what I have for him.'

'And what's that?' asked Jesus.

'My speciality,' beamed Mrs Cleopas.

'Heaven help us!' groaned Mr Cleopas.

'Heaven help us?' asked Jesus.

'That's right,' grinned Mrs Cleopas. 'Heaven help us casserole. That's Mr Cleopas's sweet little name for it.'

'So what's in it?' asked Jesus nervously, glancing at the door.

'It's a colon-based dish,' explained Mrs Cleopas, matter-of-factly. 'Perfect for anyone on a budget. It uses all those delicious cuts your less discriminating cooks just chuck in the bin. You start with a layer of colon, followed by several thin slices of colon. A touch of colon. More colon. Colon juice. A semi-colon. And then some of those rubbery bits from the edge of the colon to top it off.'

(You have a mock cookery show video here, with everything being layered in the dish. And Mrs Cleopas does a Nigella impersonation.)

'Heaven help us,' groaned Mr Cleopas.

'Heaven help us indeed,' agreed Jesus. 'Well, as Mr Cleopas said, there's no need for you to go to that kind of trouble. The bread will be fine.'

'No trouble at all,' grinned Mrs Cleopas. 'I've got one here on the shelf that I prepared last week.' And she set it on the table before them.

'Oh, to have been born in the age of the refrigerator,' sighed Mr Cleopas, scooping a chunk into his bowl.

'Let's not be greedy now,' chuckled Mrs Cleopas. 'Our guest is hungry too. Mr Cleopas, pass the casserole, please.'

'Pass it?' moaned Mr Cleopas. 'I can hardly swallow it!'

'Heaven help us!' cried Jesus.

'No need for hysterics,' said Mrs Cleopas. 'Mr Cleopas is eating his all up. I'm sure you could try just a little.'

'No,' said Jesus. 'Heaven. . .helping us. . .hope! That's the final thing I wanted to tell you.'

And he pushed aside the casserole and shuffled through the big travelling bag. He pulled out the tiny Scripture scrolls and said, 'Here it is – in the book of Isaiah again!'

"Come, all you who are thirsty,
Come to the waters;
and you who have no money,
come, buy and eat!
Come, buy wine and milk
without money and without cost.
Why spend money on what is not bread
and your labour on what does not satisfy?
Listen, listen to me, and eat what is good,
and your soul will delight in the richest of fare."

Mr Cleopas began to weep.

'Eat what is good. The richest of fare. Why waste your labour on that which does not satisfy? Oh, Kind and Gastronomically Discriminating Stranger, your words speak straight to my heart (and not a little to my taste buds).'

'Well, I have never been so insulted in all my life,' snapped Mrs Cleopas. 'And to think that we invited you to share our humble meal.'

'I mean no disrespect,' said Jesus. 'These words are not about your casserole. No, the prophet is talking about the great heavenly banquet. He's trying to paint a picture of all that God has in store for us.'

'A colon-free future,' beamed Mr Cleopas. 'Sounds like heaven to me!'

'The future. That's it,' said Jesus. 'The same God who made the world and set his people free and brought your friend Jesus back to life has a plan for our future as well. He doesn't mean to leave us wandering about aimlessly in history. He has a goal for us, and this passage gives us a kind of picture of that. A new heaven and a new earth where all that is bad is made good again, once and for all, for ever!'

'That's amazing,' said Mrs Cleopas. 'What an inspiring picture of the future! Surely you must be famished after all that talking. Here, have a great big scoop of my casserole.'

'Actually,' Jesus apologised, 'I really must be going. Just a piece of this bread will do.' And he took it and he broke it in two. And when he did, suddenly, somehow, Mr and Mrs Cleopas knew exactly who he was.

'Hang on a minute there,' said Mr Cleopas. 'He's not some mysterious stranger. He's Jesus!'

'He is indeed!' cried Mrs Cleopas. 'If ever there was a Kodak moment, this is it! Quick, Mr Cleopas, the camera, please.'

'It's in the bottom of me bag, duck. I'll just fish it out. Blast. Can you give me a hand here?' But while Mr and Mrs Cleopas were searching for their camera, Jesus disappeared as suddenly and mysteriously as he had arrived. So when they found it at last, there was nothing left to shoot.

'Blast and double blast!' blasted Mr Cleopas. 'He's gone.'

'Gone,' sighed Mrs Cleopas. 'Gone and left his colon behind. But didn't he have some interesting things to say? Did he not fill us with hope? And as he explained the words of the prophets, did our hearts not burn within us?'

'No, that was your casserole, duck,' Mr Cleopas sighed in return. 'And now I think we'd best be off to Jerusalem again. The others will need to know.'

So Mr and Mrs Cleopas picked up their big travelling bag and returned the way they'd come. Back to tell their friends that Jesus really was alive.

❓ After the firstfruit

Do you know why our show was sponsored by Firstfruits Limited? It's because, in his letter to the Corinthians, the apostle Paul says that Jesus is the firstfruits of the resurrection. The firstfruits are the ones that are on the tree first, when the harvest starts to come in. So if you look at a tree and there are a few apples on it, you can be pretty sure that more apples will follow. And the same with grapes or oranges. The firstfruits show us what's coming next. So if Jesus is the first-fruits of the resurrection, then we can find out what will happen to us when we are resurrected by looking at what happened to him.

Was there anything about Jesus after he was resurrected that was the same as before he died and was resurrected? Sure, he could walk and talk. He could pick up things. He broke bread. He wasn't like a ghost.

But were there things that were different? Yes again. He could appear and disappear, just like that. And sometimes he looked like himself, so his friends could recognise him, and sometimes he didn't.

But the key thing is that his new, resurrected body would never die again – it was his for ever.

In the same way, God will give us a resurrected body – a body that will live for ever. And it will be the same in some ways, but in other ways it will be different. Just like Jesus. For we are the fruit that follows the firstfruit.

And even more amazing than that, God is going to resurrect our whole world – make a new heaven and a new earth – and just like our bodies, some of it will be old and familiar (the best bits, I think) and some of it will be new and transformed and built to last for ever.

So let's bow our heads and thank God for the resurrection: for Jesus, the first-fruits, and for our resurrection and the resurrection of those we love and miss. And for the promise of a new heaven and a new earth one day, where we can share in God's great feast for ever.

 Thank God for resurrection

 Thank God for resurrection

> ☑ *Sketch Number Two (this sketch originally followed the first part above)*
>
> 'Now then,' said Jesus to Mr and Mrs Cleopas. 'Let me tell you a little more about hope.'

But before he could say another word, Mrs Cleopas sank to the ground.

'What you doing down there, duck?' asked Mr Cleopas.

'Are you all right?' asked Jesus, helping her up.

'Not to worry,' said Mrs Cleopas with an embarrassed smile. 'Just exhausted, that's all. With worry over our poor friend Jesus. I know, Kind Stranger, that you said he might very well be alive again. But it just seems so hard to believe.' And then she rubbed her elbow and added, 'Mr Cleopas, the plasters, please.'

So Mr Cleopas fished around in his big travelling bag, and passed her the plasters.

'Ah, there was a time,' she mused, 'when this little trip from Jerusalem to Emmaus was like an afternoon stroll. I could run like the wind in those days. Do you remember, Mr Cleopas?'

'Indeed I do, me duck. You were like a deer. Or a gazelle. Or a really rapid anteater.'

'Look, Mr Cleopas. Do you see them, those youths, running as we used to run?'

And sure enough, two boys dashed past them as they spoke.

'Indeed I do, duck,' nodded Mr Cleopas.

'Ah, to be young again,' sighed Mrs Cleopas, brushing a tear from her eye. 'Without worry or fear. To run. To leap. To fly like we had wings.'

'Wings? I got just the thing in me bag,' grinned Mr Cleopas.

'That you do,' grinned Mrs Cleopas. And she snapped her fingers. 'Mr Cleopas, the Red Bull, please.'

So Mr Cleopas reached into his big travelling bag and passed her the Red Bull.

'I've got something even better,' said Jesus, snapping his fingers too. 'Something that will give you wings as well. It's in that Isaiah scroll you gave me. Listen to this:'

"Do you not know?
Have you not heard?" '

'No. No, we don't know,' said Mrs Cleopas, shaking her head. 'And we haven't heard because you haven't told us yet.'

' "Has it not been told you from the beginning?
Have you not understood since the earth was founded?" '

Mrs Cleopas shook her head again. 'Didn't hear. Wasn't there. Thought I'd made that clear.' So Mr Cleopas turned and whispered to her. 'You're not meant to give an answer, duck. It's a rhetorical question the prophet is asking – assuming a negative response, but not requiring one. A socratic device intended to introduce an argument, which I gather we will now hear from the remainder of the text.'

Everyone went very quiet, then Mr Cleopas continued, 'Ummm. . .or maybe it's just a fancy way of starting a pretty poem.'

Jesus character reads Isaiah 40:22–26, while Mr and Mrs Cleopas help everyone else act it out. Break them into groups and teach the actions before the story begins.
Suggested actions (based on NIV text):
Group one does verse 22: Crown and circle shape; grasshopper noise, action/spreading motion – tent, canopy
Group two does verses 23–24: Planting motion; sowing motion/branch motion, blow like wind
Group three does verses 25–26: Look up/pluck stars from sky/make calling motion

'So God is amazing. He's a powerful King and Creator,' said Mrs Cleopas. 'But what does that have to do with hope and wings and our poor friend Jesus?'

'It's got everything to do with it,' said Jesus. 'If you read Moses and the prophets, you'll find that God brings hope to his people over and over again, and it all starts with the power he showed when he made the world. A God who could do that could do anything – even bring your friend back from the dead. And that's why Isaiah goes on to say. . .

"Do you not know?
Have you not heard?" '

'He's doing it again, Mr Cleopas,' whispered Mrs Cleopas. 'I want to answer. I really do!'

'Restrain yourself, dear,' Mr Cleopas whispered back. 'And just listen.'

"The Lord is the everlasting God,
the Creator of the ends of the earth.

He will not grow tired or weary,
and his understanding no-one can fathom.
He gives strength to the weary
and increases the power of the weak.
Even youths grow tired and weary,
and young men stumble and fall;
but those who hope in the Lord
will renew their strength.
They will soar on wings like eagles;
they will run and not grow weary,
they will walk and not be faint." '

'Look, Mr Cleopas!' cried Mrs Cleopas. 'Look. What the prophet says is true. Those youths we saw but a few moments ago. They've stumbled, they've fallen. So you know what we need, don't you, dear? Mr Cleopas, the plasters again, please.'

'Right you are, duck.' And he passed her the plasters and Mrs Cleopas went off to help the fallen youths.

'She's got plenty of energy now,' grinned Mr Cleopas. 'Look. I reckon she's doing for them youths what God does for us.'

'That's it,' said Jesus. 'Strength when we're weary. Hope when we've given up. The Creator's power at work in his creation.'

'Mr Cleopas!' called Mrs Cleopas. 'We need a bit more help here. Mr Cleopas, the Red Bull, please!'

'That'll be the wings then,' he chuckled. And he hurried off to help her.

'Wings like eagles,' Jesus chuckled back. 'And so much more,' he said to himself. 'Which I shall tell them about further on down the road.'

And so Jesus did.

And what did he say?

Ah, that's another story

For another day.

 Sketch Number Three (originally followed sketch directly above)

Jesus and his two friends, Mr and Mrs Cleopas, were on their way from Jerusalem to Emmaus, when it started to get dark.

'Mr Cleopas,' asked Mrs Cleopas, 'are we nearly there?'

'Right round this next corner, duck,' said Mr Cleopas. But when they turned the corner, Mr Cleopas whispered a quiet little 'uh-oh'.

'Is there something wrong?' asked Jesus, whose new back-from-the-dead body had come with excellent hearing.

'No. . .umm. . .well. . .' stammered Mr Cleopas. 'Only I reckon we should have zigged when we zagged at that funny looking rock back there.'

'We're lost, aren't we?' muttered Mrs Cleopas.

'Not exactly lost, duck,' explained Mr Cleopas. 'More like on a Happy Little Adventure.'

And then he gave her a weak smile.

But Mrs Cleopas did not smile back. Not at all.

'Did you hear that, Kind But Ever So Familiar Looking Stranger? A Happy Little Adventure. It was a Delightful Detour last week. And a Wonderful Wander the week before that. The man is hopeless when it comes to directions. Mr Cleopas, the A – Z map, please.'

But, for the first time on their journey, Mr Cleopas did not reach into his big travelling bag.

And he did not pass his wife the map.

No. Mr Cleopas did the manly thing instead, and said, 'We don't need directions, duck. We can find our own way.'

'I see his point,' added Jesus, being a man as well, and divine perfection not necessarily extending to directional ability.

'You can see his point?' exclaimed Mrs Cleopas. 'You can see his point? Why, if Mr Cleopas had led our ancestors through the wilderness, we would still be lost on the far side of the Jordan, munching manna sandwiches and gnawing on quail bones.'

'That's it!' said Jesus, reaching for the box of tiny scrolls. 'A way through the wilderness. I think our friend Isaiah has something to say about that as well.'

'My goodness, Kind But Exceedingly Familiar With the Law and the Prophets Stranger,' said Mr Cleopas. 'You do know your way around the Scriptures.'

'Indeed you do,' chuckled Mrs Cleopas. 'It's almost like you'd written them yourself.'

'Depends largely on your theory of inspiration,' muttered Jesus, as he rolled through the scroll. 'Ah, here it is!

"This is what the Lord says –
he who made a way through the sea,
a path through the mighty waters. . ." '

'Wait. . .wait. . .wait just a moment, Kind But Wandering Once Again From the Point Stranger,' said Mrs Cleopas. 'This is all about water. And we're in a desert. We're having a little problem with geography again, aren't we?'

'I beg to differ, duck,' differed Mr Cleopas. 'I believe our friend here is taking a most manly approach to this passage. Beginning in an impossible place, he will wander about aimlessly until he finds his way home.'

'Or runs out of petrol. Or dies of starvation. And then he'll gnaw off his arm so he can fight off the wolves. And the bears. And the nasty, bitey little rock badgers. Manly.'

'Actually,' said Jesus, 'I know exactly where I'm going. The passage is about the Exodus, when God brought our people out of Egypt. And the sea is the Red Sea, where Pharaoh's army was drowned. Listen:

"This is what the Lord says –
he who made a way through the sea,
a path through the mighty waters,
who drew out the chariots and horses,
the army and reinforcements together,
and they lay there, never to rise again,
extinguished, snuffed out like a wick."

'Do you see?' said Jesus. 'God rescues them from the sea and then he leads them through. . .'

'The wilderness!' cried Mrs Cleopas.
'I told you he'd get there,' said Mr Cleopas. 'Arms intact. What a man!'
'And so,' said Jesus. 'This is how the passage goes on:
"Forget the former things;
do not dwell on the past.
See, I am doing a new thing!
Now it springs up; do you not perceive it?
I am making a way in the desert
and streams in the wasteland.
The wild animals honour me,
the jackals and the owls,

because I provide water in the desert
and streams in the wasteland,
to give drink to my people, my chosen,
the people I formed for myself
that they may proclaim my praise."

Mrs Cleopas scratched her head. 'I think you've lost me again, Kind Stranger.'

'Aye,' agreed Mr Cleopas. 'I thought we were talking about the Exodus, and now there's all this to-do about new things and new ways.'

Jesus smiled. 'Exactly. Do you remember your friend Jesus saying anything about helping you find your way?'

'Now that you mention it, he did,' said Mr Cleopas. 'He were always talking about ways. Broad ways and narrow ways. . .'

'In fact, if I remember correctly,' Mrs Cleopas interrupted, 'he even said that HE was the way. Though I can't say I'm entirely sure what he meant by that.'

Jesus grinned. 'He meant that just as God made a way out of slavery for his people – through the Red Sea and the wilderness to the Promised Land – so Jesus came to make a way, a new way, for all of us, out of the slavery of guilt and sin and death to a new kind of life. And to find that way, all we have to do is follow him.'

'So Jesus is like a cosmic Tom-Tom!' said Mr Cleopas.

'A heavenly A–Z map!' added Mrs Cleopas.

'Alpha to omega might be closer,' answered Jesus. 'But yes, he is the way to a new and better kind of life.'

'If only he were here to show us the way right now,' said Mr Cleopas. 'Not that I'm asking for directions or anything. . .'

'As it happens,' said Jesus, peering over the next boulder, 'I think I see the lights of Emmaus off to the left there.'

'Oh, Kind and Ever So Perceptive Stranger,' said Mrs Cleopas, 'won't you stop and have supper with us when we arrive?'

'I'd be delighted,' said Jesus. 'It will give us time to talk about just one or two more things.'

And so Jesus did.
And what did he say?
That's another story
For our final day.

PETER AND JOHN HEAL A LAME MAN

In advance

Invite everyone to come in the colours of their favourite football team. Arrange chairs with a wide central aisle. Position a 'goal' at the front. Rehearse five team members in kit, an announcer and two commentators.

 Very soft footballs or balloons; cheerleader's pom-poms.

Outline

1st Apostles United v Chief Priest City

Part 1: Peter and John heal a lame man (Acts 3:1 – 4:3)

Suffering for faith

For Christians suffering for their faith

God-given courage

Coming back

Part 2: Peter and John heal a lame man (Acts 4:4–31)

We're never alone

Celebrate Jesus' victory

(1st) So how does a football-based all-age service sound to you? If the answer is 'terrible' or 'I hate football' then you probably need to find someone else to lead this one. I suppose, with some effort and a bit of imagination, it could be converted into a cricket or rugby service, but it would then be either a lot more boring or a lot more dangerous!

The week before, you need to ask everyone to come dressed in the colours of their favourite team. Yes, I realise there is the real possibility of serious church disunity as a result of this exercise. Congregations have split over less serious issues. But we're going to have to trust that if half your leadership supports Liverpool and the other half Man U, they will find a way to achieve Christian unity in spite of that. Me, I'm a Pittsburgh Steelers fan, which saves me no end of aggro when I'm in the UK!

So everyone is dressed in their football kit and they come to the service. You have arranged the chairs in two sections with a relatively wide aisle down the middle. If you have pews, they are probably arranged that way in any case. At the front, right in the middle, there is a goal. I'm assuming it's not too much trouble for you to get a portable net thingy (shows my knowledge of football terminology, doesn't it?), but even a simple goal-shaped rectangle, outlined with tape on the front wall, will do. Anything you can kick a ball at.

Now don't worry – and you can calm down your wardens or stewards or deacons or elders or whatever you have right now. You're not going to break anything, honest! I know that Mrs Jones donated that flower vase 50 years ago and that she was a pillar of the church. But you won't be threatening any vases, or other liturgical furniture either, because you will be using the softest, mushiest toy footballs you can find. And if you can't find those, use balloons, which will at the very least make the goal scoring efforts more humorous.

Tell everyone on the right side of the room that they will be cheering for a team called Apostles United. Their chant will be:

Jesus healed the sick and lame
Then the Holy Spirit came.
Now through his pow'r we do the same.
Go, Apostles, go!

Yeah, I know it sounds more like the kind of thing American cheerleaders would shout, but I'm a Steelers fan, remember? If you can come up with something that sounds more like what the crowd would chant at a football match, go for it!

Everyone on the left side of the room will cheer for a team called Chief Priest City, and their chant will be:

Jesus died and now he's gone
But you lot want to carry on.
We're still in charge, so bring it on!
Go, Chief Priests, go!

Practise the chants with each side. Tell them to really go for it. And yeah, I think you will want some volunteers (one at least for each side) to be cheerleaders and lead them in their cheers and chants at the appropriate time – so have some pom-poms ready!

Now bring on your 'teams'. Have someone announce them (you could set up a fake radio/TV booth up front, where everyone can see, with a mike and headphones), with a cheer for each member as they run from the back, down the aisle to the front. You can do what you like with their costumes. If you want, you can get them the same coloured shirts and have a T-shirt place print 'Chief Priest City' and 'Apostles United' on them. Maybe even names and numbers. Honestly, get as carried away with this as you like. I thought that it might be fun to have them in shorts and shirts, but also with long, fake beards and first-century headgear – towels for the Apostles, and those bigger, fancier tube-shaped thingies (look it up in a Bible handbook!) for the Chief Priests. It might even be fun to have the odd bearded woman on one of the teams!

The announcer then says: 'On the home team, fresh from a recent win over Messianic Pretender (or unlikely defeat, depending on your perspective!), here come Chief Priest City: Annas the high priest' (Annas runs down the aisle to cheers from his fans), 'Caiaphas' (more running and cheering) 'and Alexander' (more of the same).

When they all get to the front, lots of high-fives and chest-bumping. And then have their fans do their chant.

The announcer continues: 'On the visiting team, fresh from an amazing result where over three thousand new team members were added to their side, please welcome Apostles United: Peter' (cheers, runs down aisle), 'John' (the same) 'and. . .and. . .that appears to be it. Apparently the rest of the team are at a prayer meeting. Let's give them a big cheer.'

Fans chant for their side. More high-fiving and chest-bumping.

Now send the teams to the back and have the announcer start to commentate. Use the script in the Story Box on pages 130–32.

It's time for the half-time show. It would be great fun to have at least two 'experts' to discuss the first half. Make sure one of them is wearing a pair of those big Gary Lineker ears!

Commentator 1 (C1): It's looking rough for the Apostles, don't you think? Any chance of a recovery?

Commentator 2 (C2): It's hard to tell, but the Apostles are always getting themselves into trouble like this. There's some tough opposition out there. Let's have a look at what the Apostles face when they play in other parts of the world.

At this point it would be great to have a short, punchy, preferably audio/visual, presentation on the suffering of the church around the world. It may well be that your church supports organisations that help these churches, or perhaps one of your missionaries is facing some difficulty at the moment. Use the opportunity to draw attention to this, but make sure you link it to the opposition that Peter and John faced.

You could divide everyone up and send them to different stations around the church, where they can see pictures and read brief descriptions of Christians facing persecution in different parts of the world. Then they could come back together and share their findings with the other groups. Or someone might like to relate a story about how they have suffered as a result of their faith.

Then go back to your commentators:

C1: So what do you think Peter and John and the Apostles are doing to make adjustments for the second half?

C2: Our reporters outside the changing room say they are praying. That's right – praying!

 Then tell your group that they are going to pray now – for Christians around the world who are suffering. Small groups might be best for this.

Sing a song or two asking God for strength and courage. And then go back to your commentators.

Coming back

C1: Any final thoughts before we start the second half?

C2: Frankly, it doesn't look good for the Apostles. The Chief Priests still have all their big guns: Annas, Caiaphas, Alexander. They're confident. They're up 3–1. They're used to getting their way. What could possibly go wrong?

C1: Well, the Apostles tell us that they're accustomed to comebacks. They're underdogs, sure. But they say the only reason they're in this game at all is because, just a few weeks ago, they watched their manager lead them to a victory over the Powers of Hell.

C2: I'm not familiar with that team.
C1: It's somewhere near Slough, I think. But wherever it is, that's impressive.
C2: We'll see. Now back to our announcer for the second half.

As with the first half, have the Apostles dribble and score as the announcer describes the 'play' from page 133.

So now you jump in and say that none of us are alone, even when we face opposition, when it's tough being a Christian.

Then lead everyone in a few songs that celebrate Jesus' victory. And ours with him. And yeah, if the non-Liverpool fans can stand it, you can finish by singing 'You'll never walk alone'.

SCRIPT

 Apostles United v Chief Priest City

Right side of the room chant:

Jesus healed the sick and lame
Then the Holy Spirit came.
Now through his pow'r we do the same.
Go, Apostles, go!

Left side of the room chant:

Jesus died and now he's gone
But you lot want to carry on.
We're still in charge, so bring it on!
Go, Chief Priests, go!

Announcer: On the home team, fresh from a recent win over Messianic Pretender (or unlikely defeat, depending on your perspective!), here come Chief Priest City: Annas the high priest (*Annas runs down the aisle to cheers from his fans*), Caiaphas (*more running and cheering*)
and Alexander (*more of the same*).

When they all get to the front, lots of high-fives and chest-bumping. And then have their fans do their chant.

On the visiting team, fresh from an amazing result where over three thousand new team members were added to their side, please welcome Apostles United:
Peter (*cheers, runs down aisle*),
John (*the same*)
and. . .and. . .that appears to be it. Apparently the rest of the team are at a prayer meeting. Let's give them a big cheer.

Fans chant for their side. More high-fiving and chest-bumping.

 Part 1: Peter and John heal a lame man (Acts 3:1 – 4:3)

Announcer: The game is underway, and it looks like the Apostles have the ball. They're moving right down the field, almost as if there is no opposition whatsoever. Let me see if I can describe it for you. . .

Peter and John went to pray,
They met a lame man on the way.
He stuck out his palm and asked for an alm
And this is what Peter did say:

'Silver and gold have I none
But such as I have give I thee.
In the name of Jesus Christ of Nazareth,
Rise up and walk!'

He went walking and leaping and praising God,
Walking and leaping and praising God.
In the name of Jesus Christ of Nazareth,
Rise up and walk!

During this, Peter and John break free of the others and dribble the ball down the aisle. At the end of the chorus, they shoot and score. Their side cheers.

That was amazing. What a goal! Let's have a look at the instant replay – perhaps you would like to join me. *(The whole crowd can either say or sing the lines with the announcer again)*

Peter and John went to pray,
They met a lame man on the way.
He stuck out his palm and asked for an alm
And this is what Peter did say:

'Silver and gold have I none
But such as I have give I thee.
In the name of Jesus Christ of Nazareth,
Rise up and walk!'

He went walking and leaping and praising God,
Walking and leaping and praising God.
In the name of Jesus Christ of Nazareth,
Rise up and walk!

So the Apostles are up 1–0. But remember, folks, this is a game of two halves, and the Chief Priests have a strong side and years of proud tradition to call on. Let's see what happens. Oh my gosh, the Apostles have the ball again.

'We've done this through the power of Jesus,' says Peter. 'Through him and the Holy Spirit that he sent. Jesus, whom you killed and is now risen from the dead.'

Uh-oh, there's a penalty. Apparently the refs are ruling that you can't say that unless both sides agree.

Have the Chief Priests take it in turn to dribble the ball down the middle aisle, shoot and score as you describe the 'play'.

So the Chief Priests have the ball now, and look: they're dashing to the goal.

They have arrested Peter and John. And Annas the high priest shoots and scores. Goal! (*Priest fans cheer*)

It's one all now, but Peter and John are reeling. The Chief Priests have the ball again. It's Caiaphas this time. Look at those moves! He has Peter and John tossed into prison. Another goal! (*Fans cheer again*)

And before Peter and John can regain their composure, Alexander takes the ball. The momentum is really on the Chief Priests' side now. They lock Peter and John up for a whole night and set the trial for tomorrow. Goal! (*Fans cheer*) And the Chief Priests are up by two. It's just a good thing for Peter and John and the rest of the Apostles that the clock has run down and we've reached the end of a dramatic first half, where the score is Chief Priest City 3, Apostles United 1. It looks bad for the Apostles, but remember, folks, this is a game of two halves.

Have each side do their chant as the teams go back to the dressing room (vestry?).

 Suffering for faith

Commentator 1 (C1): It's looking rough for the Apostles, don't you think? Any chance of a recovery?

Commentator 2 (C2): It's hard to tell, but the Apostles are always getting themselves into trouble like this. There's some tough opposition out there. Let's have a look at what the Apostles face when they play in other parts of the world.

Audio/visual presentation /discussion on the suffering of the church around the world.

C1: So what do you think Peter and John and the Apostles are doing to make adjustments for the second half?
C2: Our reporters outside the changing room say they are praying. That's right – praying!

 For Christians suffering for their faith

 God-given courage

 Coming back

C1: Any final thoughts before we start the second half?
C2: Frankly, it doesn't look good for the Apostles. The Chief Priests still have all their big guns: Annas, Caiaphas, Alexander. They're confident. They're up 3–1. They're used to getting their way. What could possibly go wrong?
C1: Well, the Apostles tell us that they're accustomed to comebacks. They're underdogs, sure. But they say the only reason they're in this game at all is because, just a few weeks ago, they watched their manager lead them to a victory over the Powers of Hell.
C2: I'm not familiar with that team.
C1: It's somewhere near Slough, I think. But wherever it is, that's impressive!
C2: We'll see. Now back to our announcer for the second half.

 Part 2: Peter and John heal a lame man (Acts 4:4–31)

Apostles dribble and score as the announcer describes the 'play'.

The Apostles have the ball to start with. They're out of prison now and on trial in front of everyone. So John passes it straight to his captain, Peter. He's no dummy, Peter. He's using his head here.

'Now let me get this straight,' he says to the religious leaders. 'You've put us in prison, locked us up all night and dragged us before this tribunal, all because we were kind to a crippled man?'

Boom! Goal! It's 3–2. (*Cheers from Apostle fans*)

But he doesn't stop there. Before the religious leaders can adjust their game plan, Peter and his team are on the attack again.

'I'll tell you how we did this. It was by the power of Jesus, the one you crucified. The one God himself brought back from the dead. And what's more,' says Peter, 'salvation can be found in no one but him. Jesus and Jesus alone is the means by which we can be saved.'

Boom! Goal number three! (*More cheers for Apostles*)

The Chief Priests are reeling now. They thought they had this game sewn up. But in the space of one five-minute speech, everything is equal again. And, worse still, the momentum is on the other side.

The crippled man is standing there. The crowd knows him. And they know he's been crippled for 40 years. There's no doubt that he's been healed. Everyone is praising God for the miracle. And the team who pulled that miracle off, the team they thought would fold so easily, has the crowd on its side. They're a rough lot – unschooled and uneducated – but they are filled with a courage and determination the Chief Priests had not expected.

So they do the only thing they can think of – they play for a draw and hope for better luck in the penalty round.

'Look,' they say to Peter and his team. 'How about this? We'll let you off this time. You can leave here free men. But you have to promise to stop talking about Jesus. All right?'

But Peter's having none of it. He can smell victory. And when the penalties come, he's dancing around like a mad man in the box. He deflects their arguments, and their final ploy misses by a mile.

'You tell me what's right,' says Peter. 'To do what you say or to obey God? All we can do is talk about what we have seen and heard – that Jesus is well and truly alive!'

And with that shot, he scores! (*Cheers*) And the game is over.

Peter and John are set free. Their crowd cheers. And later, when they gather together with their supporters, they are filled with the Holy Spirit and the place just shakes!

It's a miracle.

It's a game of two halves.

And if they didn't know it before, they're convinced of it now. Jesus is with them. His Spirit fills them. And they'll never walk alone!

We're never alone

None of us are alone, even when we face opposition, when it's tough being a Christian.

 Celebrate Jesus' victory